Social Media for Business

Other Titles of Interest from Maximum Press

Top e-business Books

- *101 Ways to Promote Your Web Site*

- *3G Marketing on the Internet*

- *Protecting Your Great Ideas for FREE*

- *101 Internet Businesses You Can Start From Home*

  and many more...

For more information go to *maxpress.com*
or e-mail us at *info@maxpress.com*

Social Media for Business

101 Ways to Grow Your Business without Wasting Your Time

Susan Sweeney
Randall Craig

MAXIMUM PRESS
605 Silverthorn Road
Gulf Breeze, FL 32561
(850) 934-0819
maxpress.com

Publisher: Jim Hoskins

Production Manager: Gina Cooke

Cover Designer: Lauren Smith

Copyeditor: Ellen Falk

Proofreader: Jacquie Wallace

Indexer: Susan Olason

Printer: P.A. Hutchison

This publication is designed to provide accurate and authoritative information in regard to the subject matter covered. It is sold with the understanding that the publisher is not engaged in rendering professional services. If legal, accounting, medical, psychological, or any other expert assistance is required, the services of a competent professional person should be sought. ADAPTED FROM A DECLARATION OF PRINCIPLES OF A JOINT COMMITTEE OF THE AMERICAN BAR ASSOCIATION AND PUBLISHERS.

Recognizing the importance of preserving what has been written, it is a policy of Maximum Press to have books of enduring value published in the United States printed on acid-free paper, and we exert our best efforts to that end.

Library of Congress Cataloging-in-Publication Data

Sweeney, Susan, 1956-

Social media for business : 101 ways to grow your business without wasting your time / Susan Sweeney and Randall Craig.

    p. cm.

ISBN 978-1-931644-90-7

1. Internet marketing. 2. Social media--Economic aspects. 3. Online social networks--Economic aspects. 4. Web sites--Marketing. I. Craig, Randall. II. Title.

HF5415.1265.S94 2011

  658.8'72--dc22

2010017555

Acknowledgments

To our many clients over the years who have asked for our advice. To our colleagues who have provided great counsel and feedback. And to our families, who have provided us with support and encouragement.

Disclaimer

The purchase of computer software or hardware is an important and costly business decision. While the authors and publisher of this book have made reasonable efforts to ensure the accuracy and timeliness of the information contained herein, the authors and publisher assume no liability with respect to loss or damage caused or alleged to be caused by reliance on any information contained herein and disclaim any and all warranties, expressed or implied, as to the accuracy or reliability of said information.

This book is not intended to replace the manufacturer's product or service documentation or personnel in determining the specifications and capabilities of the products or services mentioned in this book. The manufacturer's product or service documentation should always be consulted, as the specifications and capabilities of computer hardware and software products are subject to frequent modification. The reader is solely responsible for the choice of computer hardware and software. All configurations and applications of computer hardware and software should be reviewed with the manufacturer's representatives prior to choosing or using any computer hardware and software.

Trademarks

The words contained in this text which are believed to be trademarked, service marked, or otherwise to hold proprietary rights have been designated as such by use of initial capitalization. No attempt has been made to designate as trademarked or service marked any personal computer words or terms in which proprietary rights might exist. Inclusion, exclusion, or definition of a word or term is not intended to affect, or to express judgment upon, the validity or legal status of any proprietary right which may be claimed for a specific word or term.

Your "Members Only" Web site

The online world changes everyday. That's why there is a companion Web site associated with this book. On this site you will find the latest news, expanded information, and other resources of interest.

To get into the Web site, go to *socialmedia.maxpress.com*. You will be asked for a password. Type in:

gosocial

and you will then be granted access.

Visit the site often and enjoy the updates and resources with our compliments—and thanks again for buying the book. We ask that you not share the user ID and password for this site with anyone else.

Other Books by the Authors

Susan Sweeney, CA, CSP, HoF

- *101 Ways to Promote Your Web Site*

- *101 Internet Businesses You Can Start from Home*

- *101 Ways to Promote Your Tourism Business Web Site*

- *101 Ways to Promote Your Real Estate Web Site*

- *The e-Business Formula for Success*

- *Internet Marketing for Your Tourism Business*

- *3G Marketing on the Internet*

- *Going for Gold*

Randall Craig, CFA, MBA, CMC

- *Online PR and Social Media for Experts, Authors, Consultants, and Speakers*

- *Online PR and Social Media for Associations and Not-for-Profits*

- *Leaving the Mother Ship*

- *Personal Balance Sheet*

Additional Resources from Susan Sweeney and Randall Craig

Susan Sweeney, CA, CSP, HoF
Web sites: *www.susansweeney.com, www.verbinteractive.com*
Newsletter archive: *www.susansweeney.com*
Online learning portal: *www.eLearningU.com*
LinkedIn: *www.LinkedIn.com/in/SusanSweeneycsp*
Twitter: *twitter.com/susansweeney*
Bookmarks: *www.diigo.com/user/susansweeney*
Facebook: *www.facebook.com/susan.sweeney01*
YouTube: *www.youtube.com/SusanSweeneyInternet*

Randall Craig, CFA, MBA, CMC
Consulting: *www.ptadvisors.com*
Speaking: *www.randallcraig.com*
Blog: *randallcraig.com/blog*
Newsletter: *randallcraig.com/news*
WebTV show: *ProfessionallySpeakingTV.com*
LinkedIn: *www.LinkedIn.com/in/RandallCraig*
Twitter: *twitter.com/randallcraig*
Bookmarks: *www.diigo.com/user/randallcraig*

Table of Contents

Chapter 4:
Your Core—Web Sites and/or Blogs   20

Chapter 5:
SEO and Social Media   27

Chapter 6:
LinkedIn   32

Chapter 7:
Facebook   45

Chapter 8:
Twitter   60

Chapter 9:
YouTube and Other Video-Sharing Sites   80

Chapter 10:
MySpace   92

Chapter 11:
Flickr   102

Chapter 12:
Tier Two Sites
111

Chapter 13:
Other Sites
125

Chapter 14:
Mobile Access   138

Chapter 15:
Tactical Ideas   145

Chapter 16:
Putting the Plan Together   157

Chapter 17:
ROI and Measurement   168

Chapter 18:
Keeping Up-to-Date   179

Introduction

Social Media has changed the way we do business online. In this highly competitive marketplace, businesses are doing everything they can to get in front of their target customer, differentiate themselves from the competition, connect and engage customers and potential customers, get their brand recognized, and sell their products and services.

Social Media and Social Networking provide us with many opportunities to achieve these objectives. The top-tier Social Media and Social Networking sites provide staggering numbers—hundreds of millions of active users, hundreds of millions of conversations going on in these sites on every topic imaginable, hours of video being uploaded every minute, a million blog posts every day, millions of Tweets daily. . . . The opportunities are endless!

When the opportunities are endless but your time and budget aren't, it can be very confusing. Which opportunities are going to give me the best return on investment (ROI) and which are going to waste my valuable time? Which opportunities will provide me with the fastest return on my effort? Which opportunities are going to help me achieve multiple objectives at once—branding, improve search engine ranking, and engage my potential customer? Are there tools to help me multitask—have my blog post automatically update my Twitter, Facebook, and LinkedIn status, all at once?

This is exactly why we wrote this book. We both work with many different organizations helping them with their Social Media strategies. A lot of people are wasting a lot of time out there; Social Networking is sometimes social NOTworking! There is a lot of confusion, and most businesses need all the help they can get to sort through the quagmire. This is also why we wrote this book. This book is a practical guide for people in business to cut through the Social Media noise and focus on building and growing their business by leveraging these channels.

There is a lot of confusion regarding Social Media, Social Networks, and Social Networking. They all have the word "social" in them, but are different; they are distinct but related. You can use different types of Social Media to facilitate Social Networking. You can network using different forms of Social Media.

It is important to understand the opportunities, limitations, and differences to be able to develop a strategy on how you are going to use them to achieve your objectives and set reasonable expectations.

Social Networks

Social Networks are online communities of people who share interests and activities. These Web-based online communities provide a variety of ways for users to interact. There are Social Networks that cater to every niche, every interest, every demographic, and every geographic region.

Social Networking

Social Networking is using Social Media technology and a Social Network to form new relationships and strengthen old relationships online. The opportunity is to find the Social Networks relevant to your business, determine the best way to achieve your objectives while abiding by the "rules," and then implement your strategy.

Social Media

Social Media is a technology type where the media is designed to be easily shared. "Social Media" is an umbrella term that covers technology such as blogs, vlogs, photo sharing, video sharing, wikis, podcasts, micro-blogs, music sharing, forums, rating and reviews, social bookmarks, and online communities, to name a few.

For ease of reading, within this book we are using the term *Social Media* to refer to all three.

About This Book

In Chapter 1 we help you decide if you should include Social Media in your marketing mix. All Social Media may not be appropriate for all businesses.

Then, in Chapter 2, we help you consider the directional focus of your Social Media strategy: Should you be a leader or just keep up with the competition? Be a minimalist or use it selectively? Your direction has an impact on your strategy, and also the size of your Social Media investment.

In Chapter 3 we discuss the multiplier effect of Social Media integration. Social Media is not a standalone; it needs to be integrated with your other online marketing and business activities.

In Chapter 4 we discuss your core—your Web site and/or your blog.

In Chapter 5 we discuss the impact of Social Media on the search engines. We also provide tools and tactics for search engine optimization in the specific **Social Media venues** (Chapters 6 through 13).

> **Social Media venues**
>
> *Social Media or Social Networking sites.*

In Chapters 6 through 11 we go into detail on the top six Social Media and Social Networking sites that provide great business opportunities—LinkedIn, Facebook, Twitter, YouTube, MySpace, and Flickr. We discuss the venues and provide details on the elements, features, and opportunities of each.

In Chapters 12 and 13 we provide information on the tier 2 Social Media and Social Networking platforms—Plaxo, Naymz, Xing, and Digg, as well as many of the other Social Media sites you may see.

In Chapter 14 we discuss the impact and opportunities that mobile access provides.

In Chapter 15 we provide a number of Social Media and Social Networking tactical ideas and opportunities organized by business function. While the book subtitle reads *101 Ways*, we have provided over 150 ways in this chapter alone.

Chapter 16 is devoted to helping you develop your strategic Social Media plan. Your Social Media strategy needs to be well thought out. It should evolve from your objectives or goals. It should be documented with the details of what is going to be done, when, by whom, how often, what "success" looks like for each tactic, and how it is going to be measured. This chapter contains the "Social Media priority planner."

In Chapter 17 we help you to determine if what you're doing is working. This is an evolving area and often is difficult to measure. We discuss ROI (return on investment), ROE (return on effort), and measurement.

In Chapter 18 we provide you with a number of ways to keep up to date in this evolving and ever-changing Social Networking and Social Media world.

Don't forget to check out this book's companion Web site on a regular basis for up-to-the-minute tips, tools, techniques, and strategies.

We'd love to connect with you online. To connect with us, go to *http://www.susansweeney.com* and *http://www.randallcraig.com*, where you will be provided with all of our Social Media links.

1

Should Social Media Be Part of Your Marketing Mix?

It's tempting to get on the Social Media bus and quickly adopt it before "it's too late." Indeed, like the rush to develop corporate Web sites in the mid- to late 1990s, Social Media has all of the trappings of a fad, replete with get-rich-quick artists, "systems," and a vocabulary all its own.

Many people back in the 90s developed Web sites that just didn't work for them because they didn't do their homework. Everything related to Internet marketing revolves around three things:

1. Your objectives

2. Your target market

3. Your products and services.

Your Web site or blog is built to achieve your online objectives. You find your target market online and then entice them to your Web site or blog to get them to buy your products and services. Some traffic strategies work better than others to achieve different objectives. Some Web site content works better than others to get your target market to do what you want them to do.

These three things—your objectives, your target market, and your products and services—are the foundation. Only by reviewing these against your online marketing options (the many Social Media marketing options as well as traditional online marketing options) will you be able to determine the best use of your time and money to garner the best return on investment (ROI) and return on effort (ROE).

You need to document your online objectives. These can include many general objectives as well as your specific objectives. Here are some ideas:

- Place high in search results

- Do more business online

- Build a permission-based mailing list

- Generate significant targeted traffic

- Improve our branding

- Get visitors to tell their friends about our products and services

- Improve our conversion rate

- Sell more in the down season.

The more detailed you get with your objectives, the easier to determine the best Internet marketing techniques to achieve them. You should always try to quantify "success" for each of your objectives. It is much easier to determine if you have achieved your objectives when you have quantified them: you either did or did not increase your online sales by $100,000 with your Facebook page strategy.

You need to document your target market. There is no such thing as a "customer" in defining your target market—get specific. If you are in the travel business, as an example, your target markets may include:

- Business travelers

- Leisure travelers

- Families

- Couples

- Eco-tourists

- Golfers.

You can get even more specific—you break these down even further. Again, the more specific you are, the easier to determine the most appropriate Internet marketing technique. In the golfer category you might break it down into members, nonmembers, tournaments, female golfers, etc. There are different techniques and different venues to better reach the female golfer versus the tournament organizer, for example.

When you have your list of objectives, target markets, and products and services, you will then look at all the Internet marketing options (Social Media options as well as the traditional online marketing options) to determine the one (or ones) that will help you achieve your objectives the easiest, fastest, and with the least amount of investment.

Reality Check

The truth is that Social Media is not for everyone—or for every business. If your business is struggling, Social Media won't fix what is broken. The shiny veneer of a Facebook page won't suddenly turn a struggling business around. And investing time and money in Social Media means that there are fewer resources available for other important initiatives. Here are a number of reasons that Social Media might not be right for you:

A struggling business requires all of your attention: Social Media is a luxury you can't afford until the basics are taken care of. Basics might include having the right staff, strong supplier and customer relationships, a strong balance sheet, and a great relationship with your banker.

Little experience "on the Web": Web marketing know-how is a foundation that Social Media builds upon. To explain: traditional Web sites are more broadcast mode, while Social Media is, by definition, social; it's many-to-many. The complexity of managing this is far easier if you have at least some experience. Many books, including *101 Ways to Promote Your Web Site* (by this book's co-author Susan Sweeney) can help here.

No marketing plan: You will want to make sure that the *Social Media Tail* is not wagging the *Marketing Strategy Dog;* it should be the other way around. Often in the excitement to "do" Social Media, the lack of a marketing plan is overlooked. While it is true that some businesses exist exclusively in the Social Media space, this book is aimed more at those with real-world businesses.

No implementation budget: The allure of free Social Media sites makes Social Media development appear costless. Putting aside the opportunity cost of foregone real-world activities, most successful Social Media initiatives use the services of consultants, designers, and developers, if only to bring best practices to bear. And if you have no implementation budget, at best you can implement only the most minimal of programs.

No ongoing commitment: Like most initiatives, there must be time and budget allocated to ongoing monitoring, development, and participation. If there isn't, then it is better to not even start; otherwise you will be the proud owner of a Social Media ghost town.

No customers, prospects, or candidates using Social Media: The old expression "Fish where the fish are" rings true in Social Media as well. As the essence of Social Media is communication and engagement with others, if your audiences prefer to be engaged using other channels (in person, trade shows, phone, etc.), then there really isn't a reason to invest in Social Media.

You just don't want to do Social Media: While this may sound like a silly reason, it isn't. Just because every other organization is doing it doesn't automatically mean that you should. Without senior-level support, the initiative will not have the appropriate priority with your staff, and likely will not have the success that it otherwise could have.

Here's the reality check: Despite these reasons, you may still want to invest in Social Media. But without knowledge—or at least the right questions to ask—you can't make an appropriate decision on the right level of investment.

Risks

Most people are familiar with the expression "no risk, no return"; these words hold true in the Social Media space as well. But many people are unfamiliar with some of the special risks that are inherent in the nature of the Social Media platform itself. Throughout this book, we will suggest ways to help mitigate the risks—but even if you do everything you can, you still may have problems: Social Media content often is not under your control.

Brand issues: As Social Media is all about the conversation, there is a risk that your brand can get tarnished, or at least pulled, in a direction not to your liking. This is especially frustrating to marketing professionals who have worked for years building a brand through advertising, customer service, and long-term performance. To have the brand blemished by third parties in Social Media can be damaging and expensive. While negative comments are one type of problem (see the discussion that follows), there are a number of other scenarios where your brand can be at risk:

- A former employee lists your company name on his or her profile, but the pictures, comments, and other Social Media postings are decidedly out-of-brand. Effectively, the employee's profile is an advertisement that will pull your brand in the wrong direction.

- Current employees participate in an online forum, and other readers may think that their views are the company's views. Even if their postings contain a disclaimer, there still will be a connection in the mind of the reader.

- One of your products suddenly gets featured in a YouTube video that **goes viral**. Great news, except the video isn't yours, and your product is being used in a way that is dangerous. This can be bad for the brand, and can create potential liability issues as well.

> **Goes viral**
>
> *A marketing phenomenon that facilitates and encourages people to pass along a marketing message.*

- Product reviews on a retailer's site have consistently rated your product as poor. Even though the product may have been re-released with all of the defects corrected, the old reviews still stand, and people still read them.

- Several comments on a job search forum speak about your company in an unflattering way. Yes—this can be another brand problem.

Negative comments: Negative comments come in several varieties. Some people have a *bona fide* issue with your product and service, and they are letting the world know about their poor experience. Some users will write stupid things; most readers will see these as they are—stupid. Others are vindictive, untrue, hurtful comments that are made just to cause trouble. Finally, citizen activism has come to Social Media, with groups and pages being set up to advocate (and pressure) your organization on a particular issue. No matter how or why the negative comments came to be, your company has a choice—ignore them or address them. In both cases, time is spent.

Personal or organizational identity theft: It is still too easy for someone else to create an anonymous email address (Hotmail, Yahoo! mail, Gmail, etc.) with your personal or company name. And it is still too easy to create a Web site with a name variation that masquerades as yours. It is incredibly simple for someone to create an identity on Social Media sites—and then claim it is you. There are procedural (and legal) mechanisms to recapture your identities, but these take time.

Advanced Tip

One way to reduce the probability of identity theft is to register "your" name on as many Social Media sites as possible—even if you have no plans to ever use them. Check out http://knowem.com (see Figure 1.1) or http://www.usernamecheck.com for a quick way to test if your name has already been taken.

Social Media page under someone else's control: Oftentimes, your customers will become your biggest advocates, forming real-world clubs, user groups, and associations, just for the purpose of developing a community of interest. These groups have now gone into the Social Media world, often developing a huge online community. The problem is that these groups are run by enthusiasts with no formal corporate connection, which means that you must trust that they will be responsible stewards for the brand. Examples of this abound everywhere: from Apple or Thinkpad discussion groups and blogs, to school or company alumni groups. On the negative side, the disgruntled can

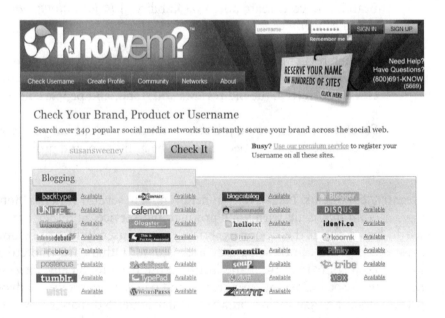

Figure 1.1. Knowem allows you to check and secure your username instantly on the top 350 Social Media Web sites.

have a group of their own, too. And they do. Check out *www.ihatethis.org,* or search for "I hate Starbucks" in Facebook. Or check out *www.ihateatt.com* or *www.fordlemon.com* for particularly ugly PR problems.

Too much time: You may find that your Social Media site is wildly popular, at least as measured by page views and user comments. Yet during the planning you had no way to know that this would happen. You may find yourself committing far more resources than you expected. Since profitability is measured by sales and expenses, not page views, you may also find that the initiative is far from profitable.

Insolvency or changed business model: As many of the Social Media platforms are free (and there are over 300 of them), there is a very strong likelihood of insolvency, mergers, and changed business models within them over the next few years. There are two key risks:

- The terms and conditions change unfavorably. Even with a moderate notice period, it is difficult to wean users from a **platform** they are comfortable with.

- The site goes down, disappears, or declares bankruptcy, and all of the conversations, posts, and everything else become inaccessible or are deleted.

Platform

A hardware or software architecture that serves as a foundation or base: Facebook, LinkedIn, etc.

Ghost town: A ghost town is what results when you build out your Social Media presence, but no one shows up. "Build it and they will come" definitely does not apply to the Social Media world; without stimulus (e.g., a marketing campaign), you shouldn't expect success.

Technology risk: It's getting cheaper and cheaper to get (and do) more and more. Building your initiative on today's technology means that you have an early-mover advantage. But your competitors who wait can use tomorrow's even-cheaper and more functional technology, effectively locking in a competitive advantage.

Downtime risk: A second technological risk has to do with downtime. What happens if a critical portion of your business relies on a Social Media platform, and the platform proves unreliable? Downtime and bugs will reflect poorly on your organization and can erode your brand significantly.

As should be clear by now, mitigating all of these risks is absolutely possible—it just takes time and resources. And despite the risks, many people still believe that a good return on investment is possible. Since Social Media seems to be here to stay, the bigger question isn't yes or no, but rather *how* can Social Media be part of your marketing mix? And what type of Social Media strategy might you best follow?

First Steps

For most readers of this book, you probably are already doing something in Social Media. The question is whether or not what you are doing is strategic, and whether you are even considering the return on investment issue. Even if you are "advanced," now might be a good time to take a step back and look at the question of Social Media strategically.

1. Define your Social Media objectives and target markets for the products and services you would like to promote. For the advanced Social Media marketer, go through your target markets (and objectives) yet again, and connect your experience over the prior year to the objectives that you have set—what changes need to be made as a result?

2. Do a reality check with a third party—make sure that your reasons for doing Social Media actually make sense.

3. If there is anything in your business that needs fixing before making a further Social Media investment, make sure that you take care of this first.

2

Deciding How (and Why) You Will Use Social Media

There are as many strategies for building a Social Media presence as there are Social Media sites. Throughout the rest of this book, we will highlight how to use individual sites and how you can short-cut your way to success. First, though, consider your overall Social Media goals. Do you want to build better customer relationships? Build a prospect list? Recruit? Lead your industry—or follow? Or perhaps you have some other goals related to branding or doing more business.

Strategic Hierarchy

"Strategy" means the overall direction of your company, while "tactics" refers to the specific action items that you need to do to execute the strategy. That being said, strategy can be viewed at multiple levels in a hierarchy. For example:

1. Corporate strategy

2. Within corporate strategy, there is marketing strategy, human resources (HR) strategy, information technology (IT) strategy, production strategy, etc.

3. Within marketing strategy, there are specific strategies for advertising, public relations (PR), pricing, sales, Social Media, etc. (Note: there are components of a Social Media strategy that may also fall within HR and IT, not just marketing.)

4. Within a Social Media strategy, there may be specific strategies for LinkedIn, YouTube, Twitter, Facebook, etc.

5. Finally, within your LinkedIn strategy, there may be specific tactics that should be followed, such as joining, adding connections, updating status, etc.

In this chapter, we are looking at the directional focus you want to use with Social Media: we're operating at levels 2 and 3.

Building Relationships

Ostensibly, the entire goal of any marketing program is to move the relationship through awareness to a sale. Social Media, given its conversational nature, lends itself very well to each part of this cycle. It provides some things that traditional Web sites do not: third-party endorsement from existing customers, interaction with internal company representatives, product support post-purchase, and much more. The more the engagement, the stronger the relationship will become— even when the engagement is with other users on your Social Media platform and not your organization directly.

Furthermore, prospects (and customers) who interact within the Social Media presence will broadcast their participation to their circle of friends, spreading your message to an even wider audience.

Relationships exist in the world of human resources as well: People move from candidates, to employees, and eventually to "alumni" of your organization. Social Media can be used to build and maintain these relationships as well.

If building relationships is one of your objectives, then you will be looking to build out a very robust Social Media strategy in order to reach prospects, customers, potential employees, etc., wherever they may be—on LinkedIn, Facebook, YouTube, etc.

Be a Social Media Leader

For those organizations that are willing to make the jump, Social Media can help power—and change—the nature of the business itself. The *Be a Social Media*

Leader strategy is to move part of the organization's business model directly online, beyond the basics of a Web site with a shopping cart and a blog. It is to embrace—and then extend—the corporate strategy itself.

A great example of this can be found in the world of book retailing. Consider Barnes and Noble. They realized they would have to compete against Amazon.com, so they built *www.bn.com*. While they see their physical presence as a strategic advantage, and in fact you can purchase books online and then pick up your products in a store, the sales from their Web site are generated in a very different way, in part through Social Media. Each book page has detailed customer ratings. Each page has customer reviews. Each page can list "fans" of the book. Each page has a section titled "Customers who bought this also bought . . ." And each page has a link to email it to a friend.

The advantage to using Social Media, at least for Barnes and Noble, Amazon (Figure 2.1), and other retailers, is that the individual recommendations, purchasing habits, and other Social Media hooks will help them sell more books to prospective purchasers—far more effectively than just showing a list of best-sellers.

Figure 2.1. Amazon and many other popular Web sites know the value of, and have integrated, Social Media.

This strategy is much more than a simple move to create a Web site that sells products, but speaks to building Social Media into the fabric of the relationship between the company and each of its stakeholder groups: customers, prospects, suppliers, shareholders, the general public, and media. In so doing, the company can achieve a sustainable competitive advantage.

Building a Following

In the "old world" of direct mail, the number one objective was to grow and maintain a qualified list of names and addresses. The better the list, the more orders would arrive after a catalog was sent out.

Over the past decade, direct marketers turned their attention to email, collecting names and email addresses of prospective customers. Email offered the holy grail of direct marketing: the cost of the email being sent was borne by the recipient, and name acquisition was similarly quite cheap. Of course, an entire industry was created by unscrupulous spammers, sending millions of emails offering get-rich-quick schemes, unwanted products, and outright fraud.

As a result, internet service providers, whose systems are clogged by this volume of spam, now pre-filter email before it even gets to your email box—sometimes resulting in your not receiving legitimate email. Email programs offer another level of junk mail filtering. As a result, our tolerance for email correspondence, even from legitimate organizations, has been lowered.

Social Media offers another option for direct marketers that is (mostly) not cluttered by spam, isn't filtered by internet service providers, and is generally thought of positively by users. Whenever a person becomes a fan of a Facebook page, a follower on Twitter, or a connection to your entity on a different Social Media site, he or she is positively acknowledging being a part of your community of interest. It is an incredibly high-quality list, with people predisposed to purchase from you and spread your good word.

From a direct mail perspective, *Building a following* is a strategy where you seek to build up your "list" so you can use these names for market research and also send them special product offers. From a Social Media perspective, *Building a following* is all about widening and extending the conversation with (and between) your followers and the company.

Minimalist—Low-Hanging Fruit

A minimalist strategy is precisely what it sounds like. You know you should do something, but you don't have the time or budget to jump in with both feet.

That being said, there may be some very obvious opportunities that you would want to take advantage of.

While the "low-hanging fruit" for your organization will be different, here are a few ideas that might fall into this category:

- Register your name on a number of Social Media sites to reduce the risk of identity theft or losing the username to some other business with the same or a similar name.

- Set up a Twitter account for product updates.

- Post product usage videos on YouTube.

- Add "Send to a friend" links on the bottom of all your Web site pages.

- Contribute to discussion groups where your prospective job candidates spend time.

- Accept invitations to be part of others' Social networks.

Stay with the Pack—Keep Up with Competitors

At one time McDonald's was famous for analyzing precisely where best to locate a new franchise. Burger King, on the other hand, was famous for a different strategy: they simply located their new franchises as close as possible to McDonald's. Burger King recognized that their products and customers were so similar that anything that McDonald's did would apply equally to them.

Staying with the pack can also be done in Social Media. Instead of looking at what best fits your strategy, you copy the initiatives of your closest competitors. If they have a Facebook page, so do you. If they are using Google FriendConnect, so do you. If they write a blog, so do you. And so on.

One of the downsides to this strategy is that you lose a first-mover advantage, and you may not appear as innovative as your competitors. But you can learn from their mistakes, and avoid time-consuming analytical work.

Use it Selectively—Recruitment Only As an Example

Younger people grew up with Social Media and feel as comfortable using it as the older generation felt about watching television. Indeed, the growing importance

Job boards

Online locations that provides an up-to-date listing of current job vacancies in various industries.

of the **job boards** over the past 15 years has trained just about every job seeker of the importance of using the internet in a job search.

Lately, a number of Social Media sites have moved into the recruitment territory explicitly, by allowing testimonials and recommendations, selling job postings, and building in job-search tools.

A Social Media *"recruitment"* strategy is one that seeks to attract the best candidates through recommendations and then to use Social Media connections to improve the due diligence and reference checking process.

Development of Your Personal Profile

A key question that always comes up has to do with Social Media initiatives at the company level, versus Social Media activities that employees engage in on an individual basis: which should take priority? The company really has no direct control over what employees do on their own time within their own personal Social Media pages. Yet there is an opportunity to ask employees—who usually are proud of their workplace—to advocate on the company's behalf, within certain parameters. So long as employees choose to benefit by communicating their connection to their employer, as an employer you do have some influence. At a minimum, this might mean asking employees to follow certain policies regarding identity theft, legal liability, sensitizing them to out-of-brand messages, etc.

For senior-level employees and company spokespersons, there is an opportunity to blog, and even to develop some minor celebrity. The *"personal profile"* strategy is designed to push out the company's brand through the connections of each employee.

How to Decide

There are an endless number of other strategies. For example, some Social Media initiatives are *campaign-based*, focused only on extending a specific marketing initiative. Another strategy is *experimental*, focused on capturing mindshare on each new platform that is released. Another strategy is based on *search engine rankings*, focused exclusively on flooding Google with search results that all point back to the company's Web site.

Each of these strategies and the ones described earlier in the chapter are certainly not mutually exclusive, but provide different justifications for your

Social Media investment. The question at this point, however, is how might they be integrated with your marketing plans, and with each other?

First Steps

1. Choose a directional strategy. If you have been using Social Media for some time, consider whether it is appropriate to change your directional strategy to a more active one.

2. Identify the lowest-hanging fruit: what are the most obvious, easiest-to-implement Social Media activities? For the advanced Social Media marketer, consider the changes in the Social Media world: there may indeed be new low-hanging fruit that you had dismissed earlier.

Additional Resources

Here are some additional resources that you may find useful.

Books

- *Trust Agents: Using the Web to Build Influence, Improve Reputation, and Earn Trust*, by Chris Brogan and Julien Smith, August 2009
  This book does a great job describing the connection between trust and relationships and how, conceptually, this can be used with Social Media to build brands and build business.

- *Here Comes Everybody: The Power of Organizing without Organizations*, by Clay Shirky, February 2009
  This entertaining book describes numerous examples of how individuals can be bound together with common *self-committed* goals. The book offers a counterpoint to marketers who have been brought up to think that only they can impact their brand—or create action.

- *Online PR and Social Media*, by Randall Craig *(http://www.OnlinePR-SocialMedia.com)*, November 2009
  This series of books takes a look at Social Media strategy from a different perspective completely, using an "anchor and outpost" model to improve reach and efficiency. There are different editions of this book for different industries.

3

Integration of Social Media

Not a "Tack-on"

A successful Social Media strategy should be integrated into the core of your business—not a tack-on afterthought. Unfortunately, there is no shortage of newly minted experts who will convince you that you need only sign up at the newest Social Media Web site and your problems will be solved. Just add Twitter! Problems can't be solved (or opportunities realized) by merely starting to use Twitter. The expression is a play on the product and service advertisements that say to "Just add XXXX" to solve the problem.

Social Media is new enough that there still is room for experimentation, but let's call this what it is: experimentation. Typically, these experiments are done in the corners of the IT and marketing groups, and sometimes in HR with respect to recruiting. They are poorly funded and not widely advertised, because if they fail, there are serious ramifications. They are *tacked on*, not integrated. Tack-on Social Media has another problem: because they are often done *sotto voce*, in the background, there is rarely any analytical rigor applied to the initiative's measurement of success.

Nevertheless, like all good experiments, they yield a bounty of experience, and this experience, both with the Social Media tools and with the management processes around them, can lead to tremendous wins. Some examples of experimentation include:

- Ask a few questions on a Social Media site about a product wish list.

- Start a Twitter account to tell "the world" about short-term opportunities.

- Make a corporate Facebook page, complete with your logo (but not much else).

- Post pictures of a company event on Flickr or another photo-sharing site.

- Add one or two videos of a product launch on YouTube.

- Try any other low-hanging-fruit activity.

While Social Media experimentation does have some merits, at some point the experiment has to end, and the real work of integration has to begin.

Social Media Integration

Each of the ideas just discussed can stand on its own as a "tack-on" or can be part of an integrated system. Consider a scenario where a new product is being launched. How might Social Media be used?

Well before the launch itself, a Facebook fan page is created. Facebook and Google pay-per-click advertising helps create a fan base, as do invitations to all of the organization's Twitter followers. On the fan page, an active moderator fills the page with interesting "insider" knowledge about the new product, generating significant buzz among the fans. One of the things that is posted is a code for a discount on pre-orders of the product. These fans then take this and Tweet about it. They also change their LinkedIn, MySpace, and Facebook status accordingly, broadcasting news about the impending product launch very widely. This happens several times, with other key news, before the product is released.

When the launch actually happens, the traditional marketing materials are laden with comments from the Facebook fan page. The fan page is loaded with specifications, instruction manuals, videos, and coverage from the media. Fans also begin loading their own videos, comments, and other information. The company Tweets about the launch, providing links to the Facebook page. And a Social Media news release is created and distributed.

This example doesn't consider how a blog can be used, user voting, or any other Social Media tools. Yet, it is clear how integral Social Media was to the product launch strategy.

Wiki

A collaborative Web site that can be directly edited by anyone with access to it.

This same concept can be applied to just about every aspect of your business, internally and externally. Some ideas:

• An engineering team can use a **wiki** to collaboratively create a support database, embedding YouTube or Flickr media within the wiki pages.

• Marketers can use detailed analytics from their Web site to determine where to place advertising. (They can also use it to make changes to the Web site structure and content.)

• Recruiters and HR can use Social Media to post job ads, as well as improve the reference-checking process.

PPC, or Pay-per-click

This refers to Web advertising where the advertiser pays only when the user clicks the ad; this is in contrast to where the advertiser pays each time the ad is viewed.

• Marketers can use targeted **pay-per-click** advertising to appear on profiles that meet certain demographic and key-word criteria.

• Sales can use LinkedIn to look for a connection to a certain prospect. And then they use their status to put out a call for prospective buyers.

• Restaurants can use Twitter to announce daily specials. Golf courses can announce open tee times. Airlines can announce last-minute travel deals.

In addition, integration can also happen between Social Media sites themselves. Consider the following examples:

• A blog can host pictures from Flickr and videos from YouTube.

• Tools exist to have your Tweet automatically change the status of many Social Media services.

• Your Web site can host comments on each of your pages; then users can vote whether they found the comments useful or not.

Quick Summary

Integrating Social Media has a powerful multiplying effect, especially when the sites are wired together. When your content is syndicated outward, it provides the double benefit of greater reach and less effort. Integrating Social Media with existing business practices has the benefit of amplifying your company's real-world activities with your target audiences.

First Steps

1. Look at your internal processes and identify which ones might benefit (or benefit further) from Social Media.

2. Review your existing Web and Social Media initiatives and identify manual processes that might be candidates for automation or integration.

4

Your Core—Web Sites and/or Blogs

The online world is very confusing for many businesses. Back in the olden days (two years ago in internet years :-) a business had a Web site and they had to generate traffic to be able to do business—nice and simple. Then blogs appeared on the scene and many businesses saw the benefit and added a blog to their marketing mix. Now many businesses are participating in several Social Media venues that need to be updated. Things are getting a little out of hand as many organizations, on a regular basis, have to:

- Update their Web site

- Generate traffic to the Web site

- Manage search engine optimization

- Update their blog

- Generate traffic to the blog

- Update their Facebook profile

- Do whatever Facebook marketing they are doing (groups, events, etc.)

- Update their profile in LinkedIn

- Do whatever marketing they are doing on LinkedIn (answers, groups, etc.)

- Upload videos to YouTube

- Tweet

- Run Web metrics and Web traffic analysis.

It's all getting to be a little too much! Let's take a look at what the critical elements are and how we might be able to streamline a little. The critical elements of the traditional Web site included:

- Storefront—the ability to sell your products or services. For some this is a reservation system or something else, but you get the idea: there needs to be a place where your customers can quickly and easily do business with you online.

- Permission marketing—contrary to popular belief, this is far from dead. Today this is probably more important than ever. Everyone is growing their fans, friends, and followers in their Social Media venues, but most are not thinking about ensuring that when the next great social venue comes along (and it will!) and their friends or followers or fans move on, they still have a way to stay in touch.

> **Permission marketing**
>
> *Marketing where visitors agree (opt-in) to receive email communication*

- Search engine optimization—it is always important for your target market to be able to find you.

- Repeat traffic—the more often you get your target market to visit, the more often your brand is reinforced, the more likely you are to get permission to stay in touch, the more likely they will tell others about you, and the more likely you will be "first in mind" when they go to buy your types of products and services.

- Great content—goes without saying.

Today you need to make sure that your Web site and/or your blog provides access to your Social Media and your Social Media provides access and exposure to your Web site and/or blog. Make it easy for your Web site or blog visitors to become a fan, friend, or follower.

Figure 4.1.   Susan's Web site provides a call to action and a link to all of her Social Media on every page.

You can have your Web developer incorporate a neat graphic with links to all your Social Media with a call to action, as seen in the picture of Susan's Web site (Figure 4.1).

As long as you have these critical elements covered, you can use a Web site or a blog or a Social Media presence or any combination thereof. Some organizations maintain all three, not necessarily because they have thought things through, but because they started with the Web site, then added the blog, and then added Social Media. It's time to take a step back and analyze what you are doing and why. Are you making it easy for your potential customers to do business with you? Is everything you are doing being done for a good reason? Could you accomplish your objectives better by changing the way you do things?

The Future: Is Your Web Site a Blog, or Is Your Blog a Web Site?

Over the past several years, blogs have become almost commonplace. Most companies that decided to begin blogging did so by starting one, and then linking to it from their Web site. This was easy and inexpensive and allowed some experimentation and organizational learning. The problem, however, was that the company was represented on the Web by two entities:

- An official Web site, with archives, newsletters, product information, and perhaps even a shopping cart. It would often have a PR/Media page, as well as a page for careers.

- An official blog site, which would dynamically give company information as well as editorial commentary.

The challenge was that, over time, the official Web site would begin looking stale, while the blog would house a dynamic (and growing) conversation. Meanwhile, Web site update costs—news pages, front page highlights, and so on—would continue to escalate. And much of the content—contact information, news, etc.—was clearly duplicated.

Our belief is that the Web site of the future will be built on a blog engine. Even today, the most popular blog engines (Movable Type, Wordpress, etc.) can manage standard pages as well as dynamic blog pages. Beyond the lack of duplicate content, having one platform to manage both blog and Web site pages means lower costs, less training, and a more seamless user experience.

> **RSS (Really Simple Syndication)**
>
> *A Web feed format used to publish frequently updated content.*

More importantly, blogs are built using a technology called **RSS**. In brief, RSS allows any content from the site to be syndicated easily elsewhere on the Web. This means that instead of requiring users to come to your Web site, your information can appear in their location. (RSS is described in greater detail in the next chapter.)

This doesn't mean that the corporate Web site will disappear; it will just become more social. It will house the critical conversations between the company and its stakeholder groups. It will still collect names for permission-based marketing. It will still have sales and customer support functions. It will just do these things, and many more, using a Social Media platform. The Web site will not just *shout*, but will also *listen*.

Content Repurposing

If the blog concept will be far more central in the future, what is the biggest corporate blog challenge of today?

Many companies struggle with what to put on the blog itself. Yet, there really is no shortage of ideas: blogs can report on the industry, company, products, people, or processes. Blogs can provide editorial commentary on these subjects, as well as first-person experiences. They can foster discussion or can be used to shut it down.

When companies begin considering starting a blog, the thought of spending more time and money makes it a tough sell. In fact, one of the most common reasons for not doing a blog is that "we already do a newsletter."

This rationale is nonsense. There is no reason that your newsletter's content can't be repurposed into your blog: at the outset, no additional content need be created. In addition, different audiences might actually prefer different communication channels.

The whole issue of news scheduling also needs to be explored. With newsletters, articles are written based on an editorial calendar. They are approved, put into a newsletter template, and then sent out. With a blog, articles are written on a continuous basis and then posted.

If you think about it, news and announcements don't generally follow a newsletter editorial schedule. News happens when it happens. It is just a matter of time before all companies will recognize that using a blog platform matches the noncyclical nature of news far more closely than an editorial calendar can. When this happens, your newsletters will change to be a compendium of blog stories, not the other way around. Content gets repurposed, with little or no extra work.

The impact of content repurposing can't go understated. Consider what would happen when news breaks, and how much of the process can be automated, as shown in Figure 4.2.

What is the impact of the automation and repurposing?

- Cost and time are reduced through automation.

- Information is provided to audiences through the channels they prefer—meaning the message gets to more people.

- Communications professionals can spend their time doing higher-value activities (including engaging in the discussion forums, responding to Tweets, etc.).

- Because the message is being delivered through several Social Media tools, there is an opportunity for discussion—improving audience engagement.

- Faster information and faster time to market: changing from a monthly cycle to an immediate one improves the value of the information and the value of the business decisions that are made.

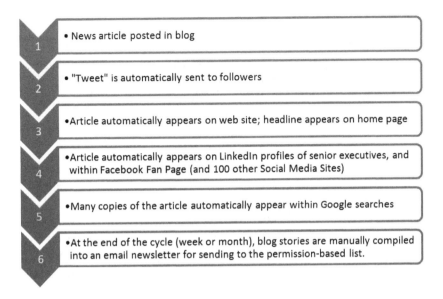

1. • News article posted in blog
2. • "Tweet" is automatically sent to followers
3. • Article automatically appears on web site; headline appears on home page
4. • Article automatically appears on LinkedIn profiles of senior executives, and within Facebook Fan Page (and 100 other Social Media Sites)
5. • Many copies of the article automatically appear within Google searches
6. • At the end of the cycle (week or month), blog stories are manually compiled into an email newsletter for sending to the permission-based list.

Figure 4.2. An example of content repurposing.

First Steps

1. If you have any Social Media initiatives, are they already linked from or embedded into your Web site? (And vice-versa.)

2. Is it time to redo your Web site on a blog platform, or is there a reason you should keep your Web site and blog separate?

3. Are you repurposing your content strategically? Plan to change the information-collection process to one that is continuous and blog-led, instead of cyclical and paper-based.

Additional Resources

Here are some additional resources that you may find useful.

Software and Tools

- Wordpress: *www.Wordpress.org, www.Wordpress.com*
  Wordpress is one of the best-known blogging platforms. If you would like to download the software to use on your own Web site, go to www.Wordpress.org. If you would like to have an "instant" blog hosted by them, go to *www.Wordpress.com.*

- Blogger: *www.blogger.com*
  Blogger, which is owned by Google, is the other very large blog hosting service.

- TypePad: *www.Typepad.com*
  TypePad offers free hosted blogs, as well as fee-based blogs with more features. Also from the makers of TypePad, check out Movable Type, their "professional" blogging solution: *www.MovableType.com.*

5

SEO and Social Media

How do users get to your Web site? While it is true that many will type in your Web address directly, and some may even have your site bookmarked, the majority of users find their way by typing search terms into Google and then choosing a site based on the search results returned. If you have any analytical software installed on your site (e.g., Webtrends and Google Analytics are the most common), then you can check the exact statistics yourself.

For this reason, there is a huge interest by Internet marketers in making sure that your Web site appears in the top ten listings—that you have a high search engine ranking (SER). This task, search engine optimization, or SEO, is sometimes made out to be a black art, but the basics are surprisingly easy, and Social Media can play an important part in giving you a high SER.

SEO Basics

The way Google (and Bing, Yahoo! Search, and others) works is simple: they index every word on your Web site and every word on every Web site. They also make note of every link going from your Web site to everyone else's Web site; this is how they magically find other Web pages to index. Then, when you do a search, the pages with the most search term matches appear higher in the rankings.

Of course, there are a few other things going on: certain instances of the search terms are more valuable than others. The page title (what appears in the top bar of the window) is more important than the tiny-sized words at the bottom of the page. And your prior searching history is also now taken into account. Precisely how the various factors are weighted is a big mystery, and the algorithm changes from time to time. No one person or company knows the secret formula, although many so-called experts claim to "know" how to game the system into giving your pages a higher page ranking.

The search engines know this type of gaming is going on, so they program their engines to penalize sites when the pages appear to be fraudulently put together. Examples of page fraud—sometimes known as keyword stuffing—include the following:

- Duplicating many keywords in tiny type right at the top of the page

- Having many keywords appear "invisible" by having the text be the same color as the page background

- Duplicating a page many times, so that it supposedly will appear more often within the search engine results.

Google (and the other search engines) also determines page ranking by making a very clever assumption: that the pages with the most inbound links are the pages that are the most likely match. This is why obscure pages rarely make the top ten search results for any given search terms. Furthermore, the more popular the site is that links to yours, the higher your site will appear in the search engine rankings. Not all inbound links are worth the same: if you have five low-traffic sites connected to you, your ranking would be far lower than if you had five high-traffic sites linked in.

In fact, inbound links are an absolutely critical ingredient for a higher ranking, more important than any other factor, with the exception of the search terms themselves. This suggests a critical Web site marketing strategy: solicit as many inbound links as possible from as many high-traffic sites as possible. Note: there are a number of other things that should be done to increase search engine rankings, but SEO as a topic is a book all on its own. To repeat, increasing inbound links is the most effective way to increase rankings.

RSS

One of the underlying technologies of Social Media, and blogs in particular, is something called RSS, which stands for *really simple syndication*. While the technical underpinnings are unimportant, RSS allows for the syndication of your

Figure 5.1. Randall's "Make It Happen" blog encourages visitors to subscribe to the RSS feed.

content elsewhere on the Internet. This means, for example, that a user can subscribe to your blog (Figure 5.1), and automatically each one of your new posts will appear in their blog reader without you having to do anything.

Interestingly, it's not just people who can subscribe to your RSS feed; other Web sites can do so too, broadcasting your content even farther. This is how most portal pages, such as MSN, Google, and Yahoo!, allow you to pull in content from other sources. In fact, there are a number of sites (Digg, Technorati, etc.) that exist only to index and categorize blog postings and make them available to yet even more people.

Here is why this is relevant: if you are clever enough to add links back to your Web site from within your Social Media and blog postings, you can generate literally hundreds and hundreds of inbound links, all from high-traffic sites. If you post your content on multiple Social Media sites (e.g., Facebook, LinkedIn, your own blog, others' blogs, etc.), with links to your Web site embedded, these inbound links will multiply even further. Then, as if by magic, your search engine rankings will increase.

There are some limitations to this technique: if you decide to reply to others' blog postings and include an inbound link to your site in your reply, some sites flag this link as a "nofollow," resulting in zero search engine ranking benefit. Nevertheless, if you have real content, and a site has subscribed to this content, this technique will work in the vast majority of cases.

Social Media Integration

With a stronger understanding of the link between Social Media and SEO, we can now return to the concept of integration discussed in Chapter 3. Social Me-

Social Media Site	Indexed?
LinkedIn Profile	Subset of your profile is indexed
LinkedIn Recommendations	No
LinkedIn Groups	No
LinkedIn Applications	No
LinkedIn Microblogging	No
LinkedIn Job Postings	Yes
LinkedIn Answers	Yes
LinkedIn Company Page	Subset of the company profile is indexed
Facebook Profile	Yes, based on privacy settings limited info is shown
Facebook Page	Yes
Facebook Groups	Yes
Facebook Advertising	No
Facebook Applications	No
Twitter	Yes
YouTube Video	Yes
YouTube Channel	Yes
YouTube Groups	Yes
YouTube Advertising	No
YouTube Streams	No
MySpace Profile	Yes
MySpace Groups	Yes
MySpace Forums	Yes
MySpace Events	Yes
MySpace Applications	No
MySpace Blogs	Yes
MySpace Advertising	No
Flickr Profile	Yes
Flickr Photos/Videos	Yes
Flickr Groups	Yes
Flickr Applications	Yes

Figure 5.2.   Some Social Media pages are indexed and some are not.

dia clearly has a role in generating awareness through improved SEO. But there are other SEO activities that need to be implemented, and SEO itself is just one part of a comprehensive marketing plan.

Social Media SEO

One of the major benefits of Social Media, if done with SEO in mind, is that it can significantly improve your search engine rankings. Not all Social Media is indexed by the search engines. What is indexed today may not be indexed tomorrow, and what is not indexed today may indeed be indexed tomorrow. As of the writing of this book, Figure 5.2 shows a list of the top-tier Social Media sites and whether each subpart of each site is indexed by the major search engines.

First Steps

1. Take care of the SEO basics to drive more people to your site.

2. Make sure that every blog post that you write also has a link back to your main Web site. This goes for postings on your own blog as well as comments that you leave on others.

3. For each of the Social Media sites that you are using, note which content is indexed by the search engines and then develop a system to ensure that your keyword phrases are included appropriately.

Additional Resources

Here are some additional resources that you may find useful.

Articles

- Google Webmaster Central—Search Engine Optimization: *http://budurl.com/chapter6seo*

- Wikipedia's take on SEO: *http://budurl.com/chapter6wiki*

6

LinkedIn

Overview

LinkedIn (*www.LinkedIn.com*) is the largest corporately focused professional networking site in the world. With over 65 million users, half of whom are outside of the United States, LinkedIn has developed a critical mass that can't be ignored. Yet, this number represents a low penetration rate, so it isn't certain that everyone you might wish to contact is actually registered with or reachable on the system.

To describe LinkedIn at the highest level, it is a Social Media site where you can build your profile (see Figure 6.1), include the latest version of your resume; and solicit connections to other individuals—who can then accept your connection request, or not, as they see fit. As a reward for being a connection, you have greater transparency into their experience (and their connections), and vice-versa.

From this humble beginning, LinkedIn has added significant functionality and is used by job seekers, recruiters, sales execs, and anyone looking to develop and make the most of their relationships.

The LinkedIn business model is a combination of selling premium LinkedIn memberships for individuals (not worth it for most), advertising revenues, job posting revenues, and corporate partnership deals. It clearly has staying power

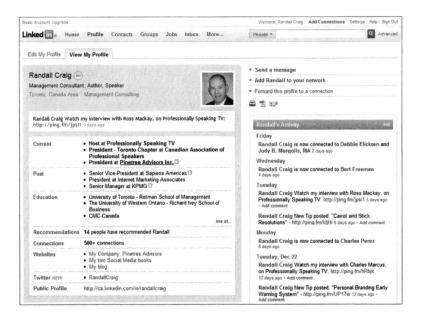

Figure 6.1. The LinkedIn profile provides visitors with a snapshot of who you are and what credentials you have.

and seems to be beating one of its main rivals (Plaxo) based on the number of users and the pace of innovation.

Following is a description of the most relevant features and how they might be used, both on a personal and a corporate level.

Profile

The profile is the basic "resume" that people will see when they click through to you as an individual; a subset of this information is indexed on Google. We recommend that you fill out the profile in a general way, as there is no need for you to put in specific job details—that's what a traditional resume is for. (Of course, if you are looking to leave your employer, you may want to do this, as recruiters will better be able to find you based on the keywords embedded within your profile.)

If you are multilingual, you can also create a profile in your other language(s). Click on *"Edit my Profile"* and then look for the link that says *"Create Your Profile in Another Language."*

Recommendations

There is a link in the navigation that allows you to write recommendations for others and request recommendations from others. Note that whenever a recommendation is written for you, it does not appear publicly unless you approve it.

> **Watch Out!**
>
> *Sometimes employees will share confidential information, processes, or projects on their LinkedIn profile. It doesn't hurt to review your staffs' profiles periodically, just in case.*

While this is an individual-oriented activity, it does have some important benefits at the company level. When a prospect is trying to decide whether your company or a competitor will win the contract, it may be the personal relationships that make the difference. If a supplier has a number of glowing recommendations, it is a powerful indicator for how the relationship might develop.

Groups

Groups are communities of interest with something in common—functional skills, membership in a real-world organization, or geography. Anyone can set up a group just by clicking on the Groups navigation link and following the instructions on the page. Pretty much all colleges and universities use this as a way to bind their alumni together. Search for your alma mater and check it out!

> **Watch Out!**
>
> *If you are asked by your employees for a reference, be very careful about giving it. Depending on your jurisdiction, your glowing recommendation might be used against you in court if you later fire them. As recommendations from third parties are stronger anyway, you can use this rationale for declining the request.*

Within groups can be found a discussion forum, member listings, news postings, job postings, and several other types of functionality. The group moderator has complete control over what functionality is enabled and who can join.

While it might be tempting to create a group immediately, remember that the ongoing management of it takes time. If you create a group with no real business need for one, then no one will show up—and the ghost town will not reflect well on you. With so many groups (Figure 6.2) already out there, it might be far easier to participate in one than to create—and spend time managing—one of your own.

One idea that might make sense is to create a group that ties into any existing loyalty program that you run. For example, if you have a real-world group for your customers, former employees, or key suppliers, then adding a LinkedIn group would tie them even more tightly to your company.

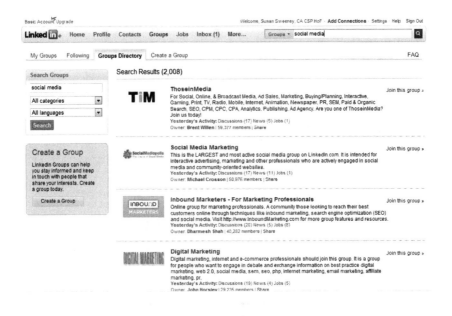

Figure 6.2. LinkedIn includes groups related to every topic, skill, organization, and geographic area.

Applications

The latest trend in Social Media has been to open up the back-end, to allow programmers to build applications on top of the Social Media platform itself. The idea is that if these third parties create user engagement and higher value, then the users will spend more time there, thereby increasing the value of the platform itself. Not surprisingly, LinkedIn has done this as well. There are about a dozen applications so far on LinkedIn (Figure 6.3), all accessible from the Applications link in the navigation menu. Some of them are very useful, such as *"Typepad,"* which allows you to automatically funnel your corporate (or personal) blog postings directly onto your page.

Here are some other ideas: Use the *"Google Presentation"* application to showcase presentations (similar to PowerPoint) about your products and services. Use *Box.net* to house whitepapers or product specification sheets, or support FAQs. And use *"Amazon's Reading List"* to highlight relevant books about your company, industry, or people.

LinkedIn Applications enable you to enrich your profile, share and collaborate with your network, and get the key insights that help you be more effective. Applications are added to your homepage and profile enabling you to control who gets access to what information.

Box.net Files
by Box.net

Add the Box.net Files application to manage all your important files online. Box.net lets you share content on your profile, and collaborate with friends and colleagues.

My Travel
by Tripit, Inc.

See where your LinkedIn network is traveling and when you will be in the same city as your colleagues. Share your upcoming trips, current location, and travel stats with your network.

Company Buzz
by LinkedIn

Ever wonder what people are saying about your company? **Company Buzz** shows you the twitter activity associated with your company. View tweets, trends and top key words. Customize your topics and share with your coworkers.

Google Presentation
by Google

Present yourself and your work. Upload a .PPT or use Google's online application to embed a presentation on your profile.

Events
by LinkedIn

Find professional events, from conferences to local meet-ups, and discover what events your connections are attending.

Reading List by Amazon
by Amazon

Extend your professional profile by sharing the books you're reading with other LinkedIn members. Find out what you should be reading by following updates from your connections, people in your field, or other LinkedIn members of professional interest to you.

Figure 6.3.   LinkedIn provides access to the growing list of LinkedIn applications.

Microblogging

At the top of every LinkedIn profile is a spot for you to put your status. The magic of this status update is that it is viewable by any person who goes to your page, and it also appears on each of your connections' Home Page. The term **microblogging** comes from the fact that your posting must be micro-sized.

> **Microblogging**
>
> *A blog that allows up to 140 character-long posts. Twitter is the most popular.*

Obviously, if you change your status too often, your connections will tire of your "noise" and will disconnect from you. On the other hand, occasional (and strategic) company-focused messages to your connections provide a targeted way to get your message to those who care about you and what you're doing.

These strategic messages need not be complex. If you wanted to differentiate your business because of your product quality, then you would insert a message every time your products won a product quality award, or about the product quality courses you attended, or when your warehouse received an ISO 9000 quality recertification. A subtle mention from time to time can have far more impact than a continuous "shout."

Job Postings

Many companies have programs where employees who refer job candidates get a bonus if the person is ultimately hired. The rationale for doing this is that the relationship improves the quality of the candidate. LinkedIn, with its job postings, is merely an extension of this philosophy. If you had two job candidates, and one was connected to a LinkedIn connection, wouldn't that person have a leg up on the unknown person?

By posting a job on LinkedIn, you are able to follow the connections between the candidate and yourself, asking "up the chain" for a candid assessment of the person's suitability and capabilities. In addition, the job posting gets spread virally, as connections tell their connections about it. The cost for posting a job is competitive with other job boards.

Most people aren't aware of the very significant investment that LinkedIn has made to help recruiters and hiring managers. For example, there are administrative tools that provide more sophisticated access to the LinkedIn database for passive searching, LinkedIn-based targeted direct mail, and tracking of applicants for any job search. More information is available at *http://talent.linkedin.com*.

Advanced Tip

Many people forget that you can put a Web page address within your status area. Whenever you change your status, always think of what you want your readers' next step to be, and then provide the Web page address that takes them there.

Answers

LinkedIn Answers (Figure 6.4) is intriguing, as users can pose questions on any business-oriented topic, and other users provide answers. One of the answers is selected as the "Best Answer," while other(s) may be selected as "Good Answers."

There is certainly a benefit to participating in these forums, so long as you limit your participation to be within your company's sphere of interest, or if it will help you accomplish your Social Media objectives. When people read your answers, especially if

Time Waster

It is easy to waste huge amounts of time responding to generic questions. We recommend that if you do wish to respond to questions, then do so only for a smaller number of questions so that you can demonstrate your expertise. Anything more doesn't get you much.

Another opportunity, instead of the generic "Answers" area of the site, is to spend some time developing a reputation within the groups, participating in expertise-relevant discussions. The audience is far more targeted, and you'll be more likely to benefit from your effort.

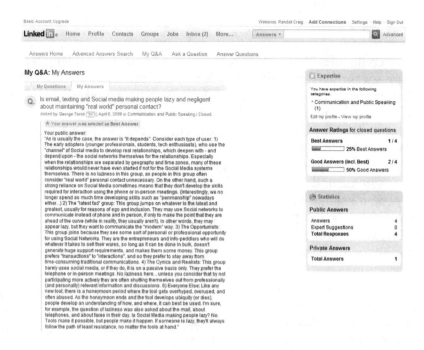

Figure 6.4.   LinkedIn Answers provides an opportunity for you to showcase your expertise by answering questions—or asking your own.

they are tagged as "Best" or "Good," there is a clear commercial benefit to you and your organization. And once the question is answered, it can be searched for (and found) over and over, providing a continuing return on your one-time investment.

Company Page

Keep in mind that LinkedIn started as an individual-centered Social Media site, and this continues to be one of its strengths. There is the concept of "Company," though; it builds company profiles from the ground, by aggregating individual profiles who have listed your company as their current employer. Then it provides a tool for a corporate representative to edit the company-level information, including basic information, logo, locations, financials, and a company blog.

LinkedIn has an option for you to purchase a custom company profile, which gives you the ability to add any number of custom modules, including video, external **newsfeeds**, careers information, employee spotlights, etc. Unlike job search Web sites (such as Monster, Careerbuilder, HotJobs, etc.), the

Newsfeeds

An automatically produced listing of blog or news headlines and excerpts.

ability to marry company information with your network data and job postings can make company listings very powerful. Typically, only larger companies have used this capability, but if your organization's Social Media strategy relies highly on LinkedIn, then a custom company profile may be a worthwhile investment.

LinkedIn Priority List: Personal

To get started on LinkedIn, here is an order-of-operations that you should follow, along with a number of shortcuts:

1. Sign up for the service if you haven't done so already, at *www.LinkedIn.com*.

2. Create your profile. A very efficient way to do it all at once is to upload your resume, using the Resume Import feature. After you upload the resume, you have the chance to reconcile or make changes before it is officially placed in your profile. If you have partially created a profile, uploading your resume might be a way to quickly fill in the rest of it. Note: You are not really uploading your resume; LinkedIn scans your resume, extracting specific information, which you approve before it goes live.

Watch Out!

Anyone with a corporate email address can edit the basic company profile, including disgruntled employees. This is a security hole that we can expect will be plugged, but as of mid-2010, it is wide open. After you create a company profile, we recommend that you note a date on your calendar to review the profile, to ensure that it wasn't changed inappropriately.

3. Invite connections. The fastest way to do this is to have LinkedIn use your email list, and then compare this list with the 50-million-plus contacts in their database. If you are using Microsoft Outlook, you can install the LinkedIn Outlook Toolbar, which can be downloaded through a tiny text link at the bottom of every LinkedIn page. Once installed into Outlook, it will upload each of your contacts into a LinkedIn holding area, where you will have a chance to choose whom to send a connection invitation to.

For tighter integration, use LinkedIn for Outlook to bring tour contact data directly into Outlook. See *www.LinkedIn.com/Outlook* for more details. If you use Gmail, Hotmail, Yahoo! mail, or most other Webmail programs, then LinkedIn also provides a convenient way for you to do the same thing. Click the "Contacts" navigation link and then find the link on the page that says "Add Connections." LinkedIn will ask you for your email address, then your email password, in order to collect your connections from your Web email account.

4. Grow your connections: Look through your connections' connections to see if there is anyone with whom you have a real-world relationship but is not yet your connection, and then invite them, one-by-one. This is relatively time-consuming, but it is a one-time-only process and will yield results indefinitely. There are other options within LinkedIn to identify former colleagues and classmates; it's worth looking at these as well.

5. Solicit recommendations: It doesn't hurt the ego to have others say nice things about you in public. It is worthwhile asking for recommendations from a broad variety of people: former colleagues, customers, suppliers, etc. The benefit of doing this, beyond padding your ego, is that it actually helps strengthen your past real-world relationships; the mere asking forces you to reconnect and brings the relationship into the present. At the same time you solicit recommendations, consider to whom you might wish to give recommendations. We suggest that you give recommendations only where warranted, and avoid the "you-give-me-one-and-I'll-give-you-one" deals.

6. Join Groups: To begin, search for groups related to your school, past employers, professional associations or certifications, customer groups, etc., and then join them. While it might be tempting to join dozens of groups right away, we recommend that you join the groups where you can get the biggest return on your time investment. To

Watch Out!

There are some people who follow a so-called LinkedIn Open Networker philosophy. If you see some people with the word "LION" behind their names, and thousands and thousands of connections, they are following a very different philosophy. Typically, LIONs hope to add as many names into their network as possible, regardless of whether or not they have a real-world relationship with the person. Often, their modus operandi is to send "Status Updates" that are blatant product pitches. The more people on their list, the more profiles their sales pitches will reach. Separately, if you chose to accept all connections regardless of whether or not there was a real-world relationship, often you will be pestered by these people, asking for introductions. It's far wiser—and will save you time—if you accept only real-world relationships.

keep it manageable, we recommend that you don't join more than five at the start. Once you've got the system figured out and have had an opportunity to assess the results of your participation, you can then add more. If the groups are a waste of time, you can always back out.

7. Participate: A key benefit to answering a few questions in LinkedIn Answers, or to contribute to a discussion within a group, is that your name will be shown—along with your expertise—whenever anyone searches for that answer in the future.

LinkedIn Priority List: Company

While the individual benefits of Social Media are well understood, here are some corporate recommendations:

1. Encourage employees to use LinkedIn in order to increase the SEO benefit the company will have. As well, the more your employees are connected together, the more your sales team can answer the question "who knows whom?" prior to a sales call.

2. Claim and edit your company profile.

3. LinkedIn is also a very powerful recruiting and HR tool. Here are some ideas:

   – Compare candidates' profiles and resumes to ensure that they match.

   – Review any recommendations, and look for additional people to ask for references.

   – Consider using a LinkedIn job posting to tap in to the social network for potential candidates.

   – Use a LinkedIn group for alumni of your company; it's a great way for people to keep in contact, at zero cost to you.

4. Much of the value of LinkedIn can come from the suggestions you make to your workforce. Here are several:

- Ask your employees to put the company Web site and blog address on their profile.

- Ask them to add the "Typepad" application, so the company blog appears directly within their page.

- At specific times (product launch, key company news, etc.), ask your employees to change their status to your corporate announcement, so that the company news gets broadcast through to their connections.

Ongoing Maintenance

Beyond the obvious task of approving or rejecting connection requests from others, one of the key questions is how much ongoing time should be spent, compared to the future return on that time investment. Of course, the amount of time that you do spend needs to be connected to your objectives and the strength of the fit. We cover ROI in Chapter 17, but for LinkedIn, there are a few specific to-do items that should be accomplished:

1. Check your LinkedIn inbox from time to time. Usually anything sent to you privately is also copied to your main email address, but sometimes it can be missed.

2. Double-check your company listing every few months to make sure it wasn't changed without your knowledge.

3. Review your employees' postings from time to time, both to guard against confidentiality breaches and also to get the pulse of what your employees are thinking.

First Steps

1. Search LinkedIn for some of your key employees, competitors, suppliers, and customers. If they are on the system, then it probably is time for you to be also.

2. Go through the LinkedIn priority lists for personal entries and for your company. While some of the items may seem basic, others are designed for advanced users.

3. Set aside a few minutes on your calendar each week to check your LinkedIn home page, to see what your connections are doing.

Additional Resources

Here are some additional resources that you may find useful.

Software/Tools

- LinkedIn Productivity Tools (*http://bit.ly/LinkedInTools*)—Free
  LinkedIn provides a number of free productivity tools. These tools help you to build your network, manage your LinkedIn contacts, stay connected with Mobile LinkedIn, and much more.

- Susan and Randall are always updating their social bookmarks with great tools and resources. Check them out at Diigo:

  - Susan's are available at *www.diigo.com/user/susansweeney*

  - Randall's are available at *www.diigo.com/user/randallcraig.*

Education

- Randall speaks to groups about using LinkedIn in the context of business development, recruiting, and risk management. More details are at *http://www.randallcraig.com.*

- Susan has ongoing live webinars and recorded online courses on this topic available through the webinars and online store at her site, *http://www.susansweeney.com,* and provides access to others' courses on the subject through her online learning portal, eLearningU, at *http://www.elearningu.com.*

Books

- *Online PR and Social Media for Experts*, 4th edition, by Randall Craig *(http://www.OnlinePRSocialMedia.com/experts)*, November 2009

  This book describes how to use LinkedIn—but also how to integrate it with all your other Social Media initiatives.

- *How to Really Use LinkedIn*, by Jan Vermeiren, March 2009

  This book has 187 pages with strategies for the beginner and the advanced online networker. It includes a list of free tools to help you get the most out of LinkedIn.

- *Windmill Networking: Understanding, Leveraging & Maximizing LinkedIn: An Unofficial, Step-by-Step Guide to Creating & Implementing Your LinkedIn Brand—Social Networking in a Web 2.0 World*, by Neal Shaffer, September 2009

  Great book that starts with the basics—what are your objectives—and then proceeds from there. This book has many great tips, tools, techniques, and tactics to get the most out of your LinkedIn participation.

7

Facebook

Overview

Facebook (*www.facebook.com*) is the most used Social Networking site in the world. Facebook has gone from a college photo-sharing and communication site to a business networking platform for business promotion, advertising, multimedia sharing, and public relations.

For marketers, it is important to learn how to use this Social Media venue, as the numbers are staggering. Facebook currently has more than 350 million active users with more than 35 million users updating their status everyday. The stats are mind-blowing—2.5 billion photos uploaded to the site each month and 3.5 billion pieces of content (links, stories, posts, photos, etc.) shared each week.

On the business side, there are more than 1.6 million active "Fan Pages" that have more than 5.3 billion fans, creating more than 3.5 million events each month.

The average user has 130 friends he or she can access in a click, spends more than 55 minutes per day on Facebook, and is a member of 12 groups. There are more than 65 million active users who access Facebook through their mobile devices.

Facebook is a site where you can have your own personal profile, have a corporate page, add friends and fans and send them messages, join networks, post photos and videos, participate in group discussions, promote your events, advertise, and a whole lot more. With the standard settings, everything you do appears on your wall (Figure 7.1), which is accessible by your friends.

Today all types of businesses use Facebook to communicate with existing and potential clients, attract new clients, and promote their products and services. Facebook is also a valuable PR tool.

Here is a description of the most relevant features and how they might be used, both on a personal and a corporate level.

Profile

Although many entrepreneurs are marketing their business through their personal profile, they run a great risk of losing their account. There are also downsides to starting your Facebook marketing through your personal profile, like a limitation on the number of friends you can have and converting your friends to fans when you do set up your Fan page. For business you are better off setting up a business

Figure 7.1. Your Facebook wall provides a snapshot of your recent activities; it is accessible to your friends or the public—depending on your privacy settings.

Facebook page, known as a "Fan Page" from the beginning. Facebook profiles are meant for individuals. Through your profile you can do things like:

- Post status updates

- Request friends and accept others' friend invitations

- Write on your own wall

- Write on your friends' walls

- Upload pictures and videos

- Use applications that are of interest. There are many applications of interest to individuals—birthday reminders, places I've been, etc.

Again, profiles are meant for individuals to socialize with friends. Facebook pages are meant for business.

Pages

Facebook pages enable businesses, associations, not-for-profits, teams, and brands to have a presence on Facebook. Pages are visible to everyone, even those who do not have a profile in Facebook. Your page can show up and be accessible through a Google search.

Your Facebook page is a great tool to interact with customers and potential customers. Your Facebook page also provides the opportunity to do market research and branding, generate Web site and blog traffic, run promotions, build your company's reputation, provide customer service, invite fans to events and manage the guest list, share information, sell your products and services, or schedule appointments.

When you set up your page, there are three category options—local business, brand/product, artist/band/public figure.

When you set up your page, you have to choose a name. Be careful—this name is important. Think about how users will find

Watch Out!

Have a corporate policy for employees on accepting clients, potential clients, and professional colleagues as "friends" on their personal Facebook account. The pictures of Friday night's bachelor party, the comments from personal friends on personal activities, and the personal videos may not be what you want representing your business.

Watch Out!

Be careful with the category you choose as this can't be changed.

you. Users can search within Facebook—the closer the search is to your name, the higher up you will display in the search results. Each Facebook user has an "I am a Fan of" in his or her profile— does your name intrigue their friends? When users become fans, it is noted in their Newsfeed—again, does your name intrigue their friends?

To interact with you, Facebook users need to become a fan (eg "Like") of your page (see Figure 7.2). The more you engage your fans, the more they feel a part of your community. Fans can interact with you by posting on your wall, providing feedback, providing testimonials, and asking questions. They can follow your links, upload photos and videos, download coupons, RSVP to your events, learn about your upcoming promotions, purchase products, and make a reservation or an appointment.

The more fans you have, the more people you are interacting with on a regular basis, so if you are going to have a page, you need to have a strategy to

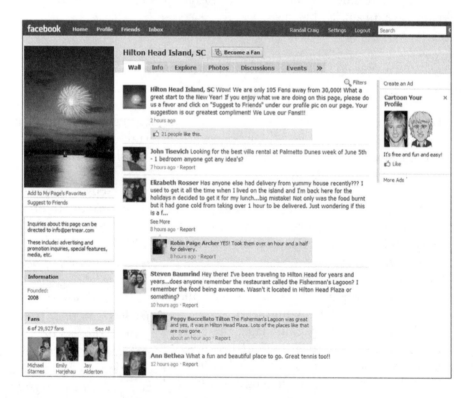

Figure 7.2.   Hilton Head Island, SC has over 29,000 fans.

build your fan base. There is no limit to the number of fans your page can have. "Groups," discussed later, do have certain limits.

You can grow your fans by offering a deal, a discount, or coupons for new fans. Whenever someone becomes a fan of your page, all their friends find out, and they are provided the opportunity to become a fan of yours as well.

Let your customers and potential customers know about your Facebook page by including details, a link, and an incentive in your newsletter or **eZine**, on your Web site, in your **signature file**, and in all your Social Media profiles.

eZine

Electronic magazine; a newsletter.

Signature file

A short statement at the end of an email message, usually containing contact information.

One of the things you will want to try to do is get your fans to join your eclub on your Web site or blog—basically give you permission to send them email—because if and when the next "latest and greatest" Social Media site comes along (and it will!), you want to maintain a connection to all of your friends and fans. Companies that built a great community in MySpace wish they had done this before the migration of a number of their friends to Facebook!

You also need a strategy to engage the fans and provide value on an ongoing basis to get them to return often. When your fans interact with your Facebook page, it is noted on the newsfeed in their personal profile, which is viewed by all their friends.

HTML content (hyper text markup language)

HTML is the computer language that describes the formatting and layout of the content on Web pages.

You can engage your fans by sending them updates, inviting them to events, or sending them photos, videos, **HTML content**, **Flash content**, notes, or posts with links to your Web site, blog, or other Social Media venue. What you send shows up in the fans' personal newsfeed as well.

You want to update your page frequently with valuable content—but don't overdo it by having so many updates that your fans feel inundated and remove themselves.

Flash content

Graphic animation used on Web sites to make them visually interesting and interactive.

You want to encourage your fans to interact with your page, as their interaction (their post, photo, or video) will be included in the newsfeed on their personal pages—which their friends can view and access. People hang out with like-minded people or people with common interests.

Your Facebook page is customizable. On your Facebook page you can add HTML, Flash, and Facebook applications to add functionality and interactivity. There are all kinds of applications available through Facebook that might help you achieve your objectives. There are apps that enable restaurants to take reservations, there are apps that can update your Facebook page with your blog posts through an RSS feed, and there are apps that enable you to schedule appointments. You name it and there is probably a Facebook application to handle it.

Discussion board

An online "bulletin board" where you can leave messages and can expect to see responses to your messages. It is sometimes called a "forum."

Your Facebook page has a **discussion board** built in. This is a great place to do market research or to discuss pertinent issues.

There are a number of tools provided that you should become familiar with. There is a tool to moderate and even block fans who post inappropriate content on your page. You have access to a helpful reporting tool called *"Insights"* that lets you see what types of content your fans enjoy and are interacting with. Administrators can add staff or colleagues as other administrators, enabling them to add or edit content to share the workload.

Groups

Facebook groups are places to find people with similar interests to discuss the topic of the group and build relationships with the members of the group.

You can start a group, participate in existing groups by becoming a member, or both. It is likely that your target market is already participating in existing groups. This is an easy way to get in front of your target market without the responsibility of developing and maintaining your own group.

If you decide to start a group, you set the name, the type, and the rules, and you monitor the conversation. You can set the group to be open to anyone, or closed where they have to be accepted, or secret, which is by invitation only. When you set the name, think about the words your target market might search on in the groups to find you.

Groups have administrators that manage the group. Administrators have the ability to invite members to join. Groups that are open to the public can be found through a Facebook search, so take this into consideration when deciding the name for your group. These groups are not indexed by external search engines.

You need to let the world know about your group and encourage people to join—no members, no discussion, no opportunity. Think about joining related groups for cross-promotion. Think about linking to your group from your Web site, your blog, and your other Social Media venues. Include information on your group and provide a link from your newsletter or ezine. Provide the link to your group in your signature file in your email.

You want to make sure you keep the conversation active in your group. Visit often, respond to questions, ask questions, and stimulate the discussion.

Groups come with discussion boards, links, photos, and videos. You can easily send news and updates to your group members—messages arrive in their Facebook inbox. You can set up multiple groups. Members can invite friends with an Invite feature. When new members join your group, the group name with a link will appear on the members' profile pages.

Groups with less than 5,000 members can send email blasts to all members. Groups cannot host applications, but they can create an event.

One of the questions our clients ask is whether they should start a group or a fan page. Our general advice is to participate in others' groups, but if you are starting from scratch, start a fan page, because of the additional flexibility that it gives you, and because fan pages are indexed on Google but groups are not. If you have a very small group, consider migrating the members to a fan page.

Advertising

Facebook provides a phenomenal targeted advertising opportunity. Combine the impressive targeting with the opportunity to pay on a pay-per-click basis, the easy step-by-step ad development process, and you have a winning combination.

Creating an ad in Facebook couldn't be easier. Here's how it works.

- Click "Ads and Pages" (see Figure 7.3) to get into the ad development area.

- Click on "Create an Ad" on the top right.

- You fill in the blanks to design your ad. You choose the destination URL—choose a landing page rather than your home page and make sure that landing page is a continuation of the ad. You can also choose the link to go to your Facebook page or event, your blog, or other Social Media venue. Next you develop the title (maximum 25 characters) and the description (135 characters)—develop a "grabber title" and give people a reason to click on your ad. Calls to action work well.

URL (uniform resource locator)

A Web address that usually starts with http://

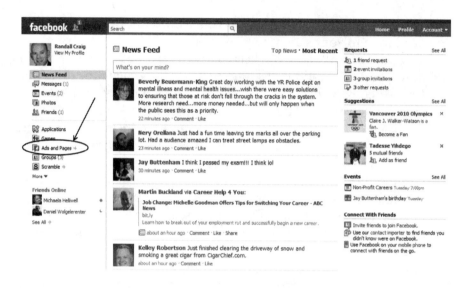

Figure 7.3. The Facebook advertising icon appears at the left of your screen when you are on Facebook.

You have the option to upload a picture or image (no larger than 4 MB). As you develop the ad, you can see what it looks like in a side panel. Go niche to get a better click-through—the more targeted your ad to the particular niche you want to connect with, the better your results! When you are happy with your ad, click "Continue."

- Now you get to do your targeting (Figure 7.4) for this specific ad. You can choose any combination of the following fields:

  - Geographic location of the user—you can go as broad or as narrow as you want, right down to within ten miles of a specific city.

  - Age.

  - Birthday—you can target people on their birthdays.

  - Gender.

  - Keywords—the keywords are taken from information in the users' profile, their interests, and listed favorites. Keywords are available

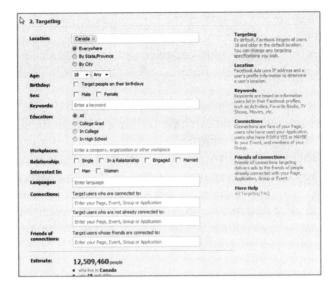

Figure 7.4. Facebook ads can be very narrowly niched.

after 2,000 users have used it in their profile. When you list multiple keywords, Facebook reads this as "or" rather than "and."

- Education—you can target by education level or status.

- Workplace—you can target users by company or organization.

- Relationship—you can target singles or those in a relationship, engaged, or married.

- Interested in male or female.

- Language.

- Connections—you can target users who are (or are NOT) connected to your page or a particular group, users of a particular application, or users invited to a particular event.

- Friends of connections—you can target users whose friends are connected to your page or a particular group, users of a particular application, or users invited to a particular event.

The opportunity to niche-target down to a granular level is powerful, and on top of that you get to see, in real time, the number of Facebook users that fit the profile you have chosen. You can edit until you're happy and then click "*Continue.*"

• Next you get to choose the currency you'd like to pay in, and then name your campaign. You can have multiple ads running in a campaign so you can manage and monitor the performance. You get to select your budget for the day—once your money runs out, your ads cease to display. You get to choose to start your campaign today or select the date you want it to start. You then get to choose how you'd like the campaign to run—either on a cost-per-impression or a cost-per-click basis—and you get to see the suggested bid. The suggested bid is the amount they suggest that will give you the impressions or click-throughs you are looking for.

• You get a final look at your ad details to make sure it is what you wanted, and then provide your credit card information.

Once you have an ad running, you have access to the Ad Manager, which enables you to make changes at any time, as well as monitor the performance of your ads.

Applications

There are thousands of applications available online for use with both personal profiles and fan pages. Some of these applications are for fun, some for productivity, some for doing business, and some for marketing.

There are many great applications that can be used to market directly; some allow advertising and others enable a business to reduce costs. Some applications have been developed by Facebook and others are developed by third parties.

There are applications that:

• Enable a restaurant to take reservations through their Facebook page

• Enable you to upload your PowerPoint presentations to share and show your expertise

• Enable you to make calls and to send and receive voicemail messages through Facebook as well have access to free conference calls

- Enable you to share documents, project plans, and tasks

- Allow you to schedule client meetings through Facebook

- Manage your rental property complete with calendar, photos, and details

- Enable you to post and view classified ads

- Enable you to have your blog posts update your profile or page through an RSS feed.

You can search for Facebook apps by visiting *http://www.facebook.com/apps/directory.php.*

Events is a free application developed by Facebook. Anyone, business or personal, can use this application to promote an event. When you create an event, it has its own page with a wall, discussion forum, links, photos, and videos. You can invite friends to the event—they get the invitation and are requested to RSVP. You can add administrators who in turn can then invite all their friends. This makes it easy to invite hundreds of people to your event and manage your RSVP responses.

There are many facets and capabilities in Facebook to do business, do more business, and interact with your target market in an engaging way. No matter what your objective, there is a feature or an application within Facebook to help you accomplish it. Chapter 15 provides many great ideas to start. Beyond these, we recommend that you search Facebook for your competitors, and see how they're using the tool and what applications they have loaded onto their pages.

Facebook Future

Two fascinating developments in the Facebook world are Facebook Connect/Facebook Open Graph (Figure 7.5) and Facebook Credits.

Facebook Connect (which is very much like the similarly named Google FriendConnect) is technology that allows users to use their Facebook login name to log in to other sites. More importantly, it allows the Web site owner to add Facebook-connected Social Media functionality, including discussions and friends, to a previously static site. There are over 15,000 sites using Facebook Connect—a very large number!

Unfortunately for these early adopters, Facebook has recently announced that Facebook Connect willl be eliminated, and replaced with a simpler, and

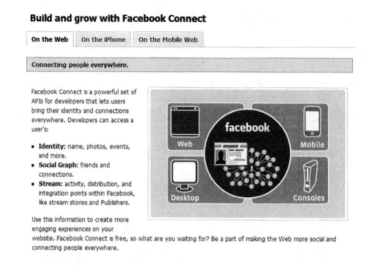

Figure 7.5. Facebook Connect enables users to bring their identity and connections with them everywhere. (Note: Facebook Open Graph will be "replacing" Facebook Connect.)

more powerful new mechanism, called "Open Graph." Open Graph allows your website to pull data and information from your user's Facebook Profile (amongst other capabilities), in order to customize the user's experience... and move them closer to a transaction. A promising technology, but one that opens complex questions about user privacy. Facebook Credits are a "virtual currency" that allow users to purchase virtual items from a virtual gift shop. In due course, Facebook Credits will be integrated into many of the applications, and in the more distant future, integrated into Facebook Open Graph—thereby allowing merchants to accept Facebook virtual currency for real-world payments.

While there is an advantage to being a "first mover," both Facebook Connect/ Open Graph and Facebook Credits still need significant internal resources to manage and maintain. Our recommendation is to consider these more leading-edge opportunities once your company has a handle on the basics . . . and a return on its phase one investment.

First Steps

1. If you haven't yet signed up for Facebook, do so, so that at least you can see what is there. Claim your name so that others can't use it.

2. Familiarize yourself with the platform, filling out your profile, adding friends, and considering how a company fan page might be used. Don't start one until you've set your strategy. Advanced Social Media marketers should review the competition for ideas as well.

3. Consider that any commitment will require a certain amount of daily or weekly updates and maintenance. Look before you leap: before committing to resource-heavy initiatives such as fan pages, consider "lighter" activities such as advertising, group participation, events, and photos.

4. Advanced Social Media marketers should review their initiatives to ensure that SEO is optimized on each page that is indexed by the search engines.

5. Set your privacy controls so that only what you want to be exposed actually *is* exposed.

Additional Resources

Here are some additional resources that you may find useful.

Software/Tools

- Facebook Polls (*http://apps.facebook.com/realpolls*)—Free
  Create a poll for your Facebook profile or page in order to see what your friends or fans are thinking. Test out a new product idea, measure the level of interest for a change to a menu item, or gain feedback on your customer service. Polls are easy to create and easy for fans and friends to answer.

- Facebook Grader (*http://facebook.grader.com*)—Free
  Facebook Grader allows you to see how your Facebook page measures up. Facebook Grader can also be used to grade a personal profile. This tool can help you determine your reach and ranking among Facebook pages.

- Vitrue Fan Management System (*http://vitrue.com/vitrue-fms*)—Free
  A Facebook application suite that can manage multiple locations or product lines for your business. This application suite allows individual

Facebook URLs in order to provide targeted marketing for each location. Detailed analytics are provided in order to monitor traffic and measure results. Manage all of your business's fans with one central application. Also check out vitrue's Facebook applications, including trivia, status updater, polling, mailing list, slide show, couponing, sweepstakes, and more.

- Votigo *(http://votigo.com)*—Fee-based
  Create a photo, video, or essay sweepstakes contest to be used with your Facebook Page. Votigo creates a branded application for your page to engage Facebook users, build your customer database, and spread the word about your business. The service also provides detailed analytics regarding contest entrants and moderation services.

- Susan and Randall are always updating their social bookmarks with great tools and resources. Check them out at Diigo:

  - Susan's are available at *www.diigo.com/user/susansweeney*.

  - Randall's are available at *www.diigo.com/user/RandallCraig*.

Education

- Susan has ongoing live webinars and recorded online courses on this topic available through the webinars and online store at her site, *http://www.susansweeney.com*, and provides access to others' courses on the subject through her online learning portal, eLearningU, at *http://www.elearningu.com*.

- Randall delivers workshops and webinars on this and related Social Media topics, all available at *www.RandallCraig.com*.

Articles

- *Mashable's Facebook Guidebook (http://mashable.com/guidebook/facebook)*
  A great resource for up-to-date articles and guides for Facebook. Covers the basics, applications, and advanced topics and also has a designated section of articles for those using Facebook for business.

- *The Facebook Marketing Toolbox: 100 Tools and Tips to Tap the Facebook Customer Base (http://bit.ly/FBMarketingToolbox)*

A great article by the Inside CRM editors with links to other articles, tools, and resources related to using Facebook for business.

Books

- *Facebook for Dummies*, 2nd Edition, by Leah Pearlman and Carolyn Abram

  This book has 360 pages of tips and tricks for promoting your business and staying connected with Facebook. It includes step-by-step instructions for creating a profile, changing privacy settings, joining groups, adding friends, adding applications, and uploading photos or videos. Authored by two Facebook employees, this book is a great way for beginners to learn the ins and outs of Facebook.

- *I'm on Facebook—Now What?: How to Get Personal, Business, and Professional Value from Facebook,* by Robert Scoble, Jason Alba, and Jesse Stay

  Develop a strategy to get the most value from your Facebook account. The book covers commonly asked questions, common mistakes, privacy, applications, and more.

8

Twitter

$\mathbf{W}$e already touched on the concept of microblogging earlier, but Twitter was the first, and the most well known, of this type of service. Twitter allows up to 140 characters per message posted, which is the number of characters in the first sentence above, and in this sentence. Without using abbreviations, most people are quite good at putting a complete thought into each of their "Tweets." (Another 140 characters.)

What Twitter Is . . . and Isn't

Many people (and companies) have misguided views as to what Twitter is, and what it isn't. To be clear:

- It is not a stream-of-consciousness diary that goes unedited from brain to post. Each post reflects your company's brand, and your personal reputation. It must be well considered before it is posted online.

- It is not a platform for ranting, general complaints, or negativity. Nor is it a platform for promises of performance or corporate commitments. Like everything on the internet, what is posted endures forever. And because of the public nature of the posts, anyone can see them, at any time in the future.

- It is not a substitute for private communication: everything that you post is open for all to see. (While there is the concept of direct messaging, it is too easy to inadvertently send a private message everywhere.)

- It is not "everything" and it is not completely ubiquitous. Not everyone uses it, and while it does seem to have a vernacular all its own, at best Twitter is only one slice of a comprehensive marketing plan.

- It is easy to start using, yet hard to manage. Because the concept is so simple, sign-up is easy, and the price is free, the barriers to entry are very low. One challenge, however, is that it takes time—something that most people have very little of. In addition, once the number of followers (and the number you follow) begins increasing, it becomes more difficult to manage efficiently. While Twitter Lists, and programs like HootSuite, Seesmic, or TweetDeck can help, most novices are completely unaware of these tools, let alone how to use them.

Interestingly, Twitter (Figure 8.1) was started with one thing in mind ("What are you doing now?") and has morphed into something else: a way to learn immediately what the world might be thinking about any particular subject. It has become a most powerful tool for marketers, providing an instant gauge

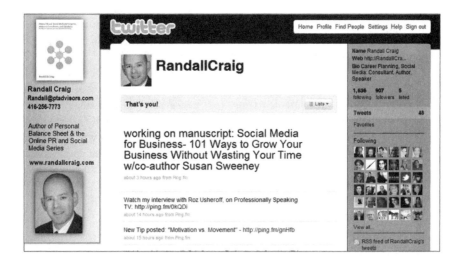

Figure 8.1. Twitter provides you access to your followers for updates, research, promotion, and a whole lot more.

on brand sentiment, instant market research, and a two-way communications channel.

One of the fundamental differences between Twitter and the microblogging capabilities of LinkedIn, Facebook, MySpace, and others is that Twitter uses the concept of "*Follower*," instead of "*Connection/Friend*." With Facebook and LinkedIn, for example, if someone wants to connect with you, they need to ask and you have to approve. With Twitter, if you can find someone, you can *follow* him or her, even without approval, unless the user has managed the privacy settings to have followers require approval.

While this might seem a bit risky, it isn't, as there is no private information shown on Twitter, especially when compared to LinkedIn (your resume) or Facebook (your family photos). All people see is your history of status updates.

The issue, however, is whether you need to be on Twitter at all, and if so, how to use it to accomplish some of your objectives. The following table (Figure 8.2) gives some perspective on the first question.

Another consideration is the competitive one. Are your competitors on Twitter? Can you determine how they're using it? If they have figured out how to gain a benefit, you might consider copying them. (Recall the Burger King strategy from Chapter 2.)

Pros	Cons
• Very quick and informal. • Allows you to see what is happening, real-time, with customers, suppliers, and in the marketplace. • Early-mover advantage: by developing a reputation in the *Twitterverse,* you are creating a sustainable advantage that your competitors will not be able to match. • It's another communications channel: if your customers, suppliers, or the media are using it, then you should provide them the information they need in the format they want. (This is the same rationale for not using Telex: since no one is using it anymore, you don't either.)	• Tough to get the right people to follow you. • For many of your customers, suppliers, and others, Twitter is on the leading edge; they're not using it yet. • Twitter is yet another "non-core" activity that takes more of your time each day. • Because of the immediacy of Twitter, there may be an expectation that you monitor it frequently; if so, it will be disruptive. • Often, people whom you follow will bombard you with spam.

Figure 8.2. Pros and cons of Twitter.

Twitter Strategies

If you are just getting into Twitter—or have been using it without much success—consider the following eight different strategies, adapted from Randall Craig's *Make It Happen Tipsheet* (*www.RandallCraig.com*).

Negative Strategies

- Time-waster: You have followed others who provide a steady stream of low-value information, but which you find fascinating. And in turn, you provide your followers the minute details of whatever happens to be on your mind.

- Spammer: Your number one goal as a spammer is to collect followers and then send links to a product or service sales page, often several times each day. In the same way that email spam is unappreciated, following this strategy is a quick way to get "unfollowed."

- False prophet: This strategy is one where you will try to establish "authority" by virtue of the quality of your posts, but where there is little or no real-world expertise. (Unfortunately for everyone in the Twitterverse, real-life trusted gurus are often too busy to actually implement a trusted guru strategy, clearing the way for false prophets.)

> **Watch Out!**
>
> *Aggressive marketing departments that are not experienced with Twitter can easily fall into this category of activity.*

Positive Strategies

- Lurker: In this strategy, you are a consumer of information. You have followed a number of people (friends, family, colleagues, and a few experts), and they provide you with intelligence relevant to your work and personal life. You rarely Tweet yourself. At a company level, this strategy would be useful to follow your competitors, suppliers, and customers. During the sales process, it might be useful to follow the decision makers at prospective customers as well.

- Searcher: You don't follow many people, but you use the Twitter Search functionality to review trending topics and links to newly available resources. You typically don't post much at all: Twitter Search is your new version of Google.

- Strategic sender: With this strategy, you send updates—usually self-centered—to let your customers, colleagues, and suppliers know about your important activities or initiatives. You may do an update once or twice weekly—not too often, or your Tweets may look like spam. You may be a lurker as well. Different businesses might be strategic senders in different ways: a restaurant might send out the daily special, a travel company might send out a link to last-minute travel deals, and a manufacturer might send out notifications on product availability.

- Asker: As an asker, you are concerned about what your customers, prospects, and the Twitterverse think. Instead of telling the world something (e.g., "Just launched the Gismo-212, find out more here"), you ask them for their opinion instead (e.g., "Anyone using our new Gismo-212? What do you think?"). While it sounds like market research, it is really more about the conversation than the data collection.

- Trusted guru: A trusted guru is a person who is completely up-to-date in his or her area of expertise and shares this by Tweeting several times daily, with links, short editorial comments, and other value-added content. The trusted guru rarely Tweets about personal activities.

- Promoted Tweets: Like Facebook and other Social Media platforms, Twitter is also experimenting with embedded advertising. It is still uncertain whether this is a great opportunity for small and medium sized businesses or a waste of time. Currently, organizations like Best Buy, Sony and Red Bull are testing the platform for advertising. Our recommendation is to let the early adaptors test the platform, monitor the results and studies and then make an informed decision. If you are investing in Social Media Advertising in the short term you might stick with Facebook and other Social Media venues that have a track record.

Twitter Lists

One of the more intriguing abilities of Twitter is the ability to create subgroups of your followers, which Twitter calls *Lists*. You might wish to do this if you have a large number of followers, each with different attributes. One list might be personal; another list might be professional. Or one might have to do with your industry, while another might have to do with your functional area of expertise.

Recommendation

Unless you have a large number of followers, don't waste your time creating

To create a new list, click on the link that says "*new list*" in the right-hand margin of your home page, and then follow the instructions. One of your choices will be to make the list public or private: remember that if it is a public list, then others can choose to follow it; if it's private, only you can add names.

This also works in reverse. If there are lists that others create that might be interesting to you, why not choose to follow those lists? It's a lot more convenient than following all of the individuals on each of the lists one-by-one.

Twitter Search/Twitter Trends

One of the most useful parts of Twitter is the real-time search capability (Figure 8.3). When you search on a term, the results have just then been posted. Interestingly, when there is breaking news anywhere in the world, the fastest way to find out what is happening is to search Twitter.

The Search entry box can be found in the right-hand side of your Twitter home page, or by going to *http://search.twitter.com*.

Interestingly, the Tweets can be aggregated by hashtags to get a sense of what subjects are currently trending. A few of the top trending subjects are also

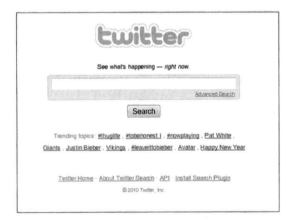

Figure 8.3. Twitter Search provides you with access to the latest-breaking news as well as topics of interest to you.

Geek Speak

There are a number of Twitter words that you may not have heard before. Here's what they mean:

• **@name:** *Each person has a unique username. When the @name (such as @randallcraig or @susansweeney) is put within a Tweet, a copy of that message appears in that person's account.*

• **DM, direct message:** *This is a special Tweet that goes to one (or more) specific people privately; this contrasts to regular Tweets, which are 100 percent public.*

• *Hashtags ("#"): Hashtags are a shorthand to allow people to search on a particular topic. If you search on #oprah, for example, it will bring up all posts that have the #oprah hashtag.*

• *RT, retweet: Whenever a person forwards a Tweet onward, an RT provides attribution to the original poster.*

• *Tweeple, Tweeps: Twitter users; people who have Twitter accounts.*

• *Tweet: A Tweet is a Twitter posting; maximum 140 characters.*

• *Twitterverse (short for "Twitter universe"): The collective Tweets and the people who send them. (The term "Blogosphere" refers to all of the blog postings and bloggers.)*

shown in the right-hand side of your Twitter home page, but there are Web sites that will aggregate the trends and provide far more robust reporting. Check out *www. WhatTheTrend.com* as an example.

Twitter Management Tools

There are a number of Twitter tools—typically, Web sites—that help you categorize incoming Tweets by subject and manage accounts or direct messages, etc. The most common are TweetDeck, Seesmic, HootSuite, and Twhirl.

TweetDeck.com: TweetDeck (Figure 8.4) fully integrates several microblogging platforms (Facebook, MySpace, and Twitter) at once, allowing you to organize followers/friends into groups, follow saved searches, manage spam, etc. There is a version for the iPhone as well, allowing for mobile updates.

Seesmic.com (Figure 8.5): This tool is almost identical to TweetDeck, with the primary differentiator being better Facebook integration. It is available on the Web and as a desktop program.

HootSuite.com: Like TweetDeck and Seesmic, HootSuite (Figure 8.6) is also incredibly full-featured. What differentiates Hootsuite is that it is built for multiple users, each managing several different Twitter accounts simultaneously. Like TweetDeck, this program allows for saved searches, groups, etc., but at the time of publication doesn't have full Facebook/MySpace integration. (It does have blog integration, and you can do multiple simultaneous updates through integration with ping.fm.)

One of the best features that HootSuite offers is the "Send Later" feature. This allows you to schedule your Tweets or Facebook postings to appear at a designated time in the future; you can enter in your postings for the week or

Figure 8.4. TweetDeck provides a great dashboard of your Twitter activities as well as Twitter management and organization tools.

Figure 8.5. Seesmic is another tool providing Twitter management and organization.

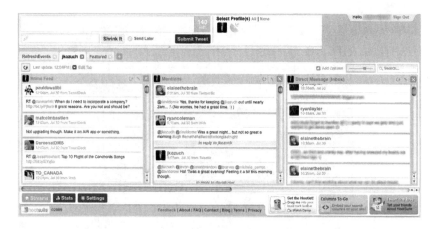

Figure 8.6. HootSuite is a Twitter management and organization tool built for multiple users, each managing several different Twitter accounts simultaneously.

even for the month in one day, and HootSuite will automatically update your accounts at the times you've set.

Recommendation

You can't go wrong with Tweet-Deck, Seesmic, or HootSuite, but there is a learning curve. Hold off until you feel comfortable and are willing to invest the time for learning the application.

Twhirl.org (Figure 8.7): This tool is a desktop program that looks more like an instant messaging program, rather than a complete dashboard. It is not useful for research since there are no saved searches. Finally, why download a program when it is easier to go to a Web site and access the functionality there? Not recommended.

URL Shorteners

One of the problems with Twitter is the 140-character limit. While most people can comfortably put one idea within this limit, by the time you add a Web site address, you are well past this limit. And with more sites having exceptionally long URLs, this problem is bound to get worse.

The solution, which most people have seen many times, is to use a URL-shortening service. Twitter has built-in automatic support for bit.ly (Figure 8.8), one of the more popular services. If you Tweet with an unshortened URL, it is automatically shortened using a bit.ly address. If you wish to use a different shortener, you can manually shorten the URL at any of the following sites: Tinyurl.com, Budurl.com, Bit.ly, Is.gd, tr.im, and many others.

Figure 8.7. Twhirl is a desktop application for Twitter.

Figure 8.8. bit.ly is one of the more popular URL shorteners with tracking features and custom-name capability.

Essentially, you go to one of these sites, paste in your (full) URL, and the site provides an abbreviated shorter URL. When the user clicks that shortened URL, the browser is redirected to the original, longer Web site. One reason for taking this extra step, instead of relying on Twitter's built-in bit.ly shortening system, is that some of these sites can provide detailed analytics and may allow for a custom shortened name: Twitter doesn't do either.

In addition to the aforementioned shorteners, many of the Social Media platforms—Facebook and Google specifically—also have their own (fb.me and goo.gl, respectively).

One of the ancillary benefits of URL shorteners is that if someone is typing in a URL manually, it is far easier to do without making a transcription error. Compare the following two examples: which is easier to type in to a browser?

http://www.google.com/search?hl=en&safe=off&client=firefox-a&rls=org. mozilla%3Aen-US%3Aofficial&num=50&q=%22Randall+craig%22+% 22social+media%22&btnG=Search&aq=f&oq=&aqi=

or   *http://bit.ly/rcraig*

There are several downsides, however, when using these services.

Name recognition: Although lengthy, a standard URL does provide important information to the user: the site name, perhaps a descriptive directory, and maybe even a clue as to the content that is behind the link. A shortened URL, on the other hand, does none of this. A possible result might be that the reader/user does not click through. Some of the URL shorteners, however, do allow you to choose the shortened link name, as was the case in the preceding example.

Geek Speak

Your Webmaster will want to choose a service that does a 301 redirect, NOT a 302 redirect. As the time of writing, all of the URL shorteners noted above use the more favorable 301 redirect technique.

We recommend that whenever possible, you manually choose the shortened link name, which means going directly to the link-shortening site and not having Twitter do it for you. Despite the short amount of extra time this will take, doing so will improve click-through, while possibly giving you a branding boost.

Note that bit.ly Pro (and several others) has a solution that allows you to use its technology, but your own shortened name. New York Times, for example, uses the shortened name *nyti.ms*.

No SEO benefit. As discussed previously, inbound links to your site have a dramatic impact on SEO. But what happens with links from shortened URLs?

After all, the link actually is from a third-party site. While it is beyond the scope of this book to delve into the technology behind the internet, in short, there are two ways that these shortening services "redirect" the link to your site: one where you benefit, and the other where you don't.

Each URL-shortening service can choose how to handle these redirects, and their decisions are constantly changing. Here's our advice: ask your tech person to look into it.

Risk of shutdown: Each URL shortener is used by tens of thousands of people each day. In fact, the entire internet is filled with tens of millions of shortened URLs. What would happen if one of these services closed up shop tomorrow? If this were to happen, the internet would be filled with bad links—on Web sites, in emails, and in Tweets. And there would be bad links printed in books, magazines, brochures, and advertisements. While this seems like a remote possibility at best, it is a *bona fide* business risk, and it has happened.

In the late summer of 2009, tr.im announced it was closing, which caused great concern among its user base. They are now going "open source" and supposedly will still operate, but this was a major wake-up call to the internet and Social Media community. Time will tell whether tr.im will survive. Then, in late fall of 2009, cli.gs announced that it would shut down. A few days later, it announced that it might not shut down if a buyer is found. We expect that other URL shorteners will also make similar announcements over the next few years—again, it is a real business risk.

The URL-shortening industry is trying to determine how to solve this problem technically, using an organization called 301works.org. In the case of a URL shortener's insolvency, it is uncertain what degree of disruption will take place—but there will be disruption.

Twitter Tips

Custom backgrounds: You may be interested in understanding how some people and organizations have very sophisticated backgrounds on their Twitter page, while others seem to look . . . standard.

If you want to change your background, click the "*Settings*" button on the top navigation of your Twitter page, and you can make modifications there. A graphic designer can even put together a custom background for you, if you wish. If you don't have a designer, check out *www.twitbacks.com* (Figure 8.9).

Figure 8.9. Susan's custom background was developed with Twitbacks.

This site will guide you through the process of creating a custom background, and will even upload it for you. (Check out @randallcraig and @susansweeney. Both use custom backgrounds—Susan's is from Twitbacks.com.)

Aside from custom backgrounds, you can also adjust the appearance of your page through the Twitter account settings. In this section the colors of your text, links, side banner, and background can easily be adjusted to match your brand.

Widgets: Have you ever thought of having your Tweets automatically appear on your company's Web site? While not always appropriate, it is something that can be done easily using a widget. A widget is several special lines of html code that your Webmaster inserts on one of your Web pages; just about every Social Media site provides them. When the home page is loaded into someone's browser, these special lines of html code retrieve your Tweets and display them on the page within a box. There are widgets to place Twitter content onto your Web site or within Facebook or MySpace. Just go to the bottom of any Twitter page and click on "Goodies." There should be a link on that page for Twitter's widgets. This is where your programmer can get those lines of html code.

Widget

Short for "window gadget," it is a bit of HTML code that is provided to Webmasters to "pull in" content or functionality from another site.

Attracting Followers

The number of followers that you have is an indication of your influence within the Twitterverse. For this reason, the collection of followers is something that is a priority task for most.

Here are some ideas that can help you to grow your list:

1. Follow relevant people; most will follow you back.

   If you want to follow us, our Twitter addresses are @randallcraig and @susansweeney. One great way to find Twitter users who might be interested in your products, services, or industry is to use a source like Twellow (*http://www.twellow.com*)—an online Yellow Pages for Twitter. This way, you can search for users who mention a particular industry (for example, dog grooming) in a particular geographic area. Twellow will provide you with a list of results, from which you can then select users to follow. Using an online source such as Twellow can help you to build a more-targeted follower base.

   > **Watch Out!**
   >
   > *There are services that claim to build the number of your followers by indiscriminately following others who they know will follow you back. If you go this route, you will likely attract followers who are spammers, each of whom sends you spam several times daily. It's better to build your list organically*

   When registering, it may be a good idea to use an email address such as socialmedia@yourdomain.com. That way, if the person who currently manages your account changes departments or leaves the company, the account doesn't go with him or her.

2. Put your @name Twitter address wherever you put your email address. For example:

   - In your email signature

   - On your business cards

   - On your corporate stationery

   - In your advertising

   - On product packaging

Figure 8.10. Susan provides a link to all her Social Media applications from every page of her Web site.

- In press releases

- On your Web site (Figure 8.10).

3. Respond to others' Twitter questions.

4. Retweet other people's messages.

5. Mention your @name in your presentations.

6. Use widgets on your Web site to display your Tweets.

7. Don't be crassly self-promotional, or your most valuable followers will desert you.

Finally, remember that it takes time to build your followers. As your followers become comfortable with and interested in your valuable Tweets, they will begin to forward them to their own followers, amplifying your message significantly. As more people choose to sign up for Twitter, the opportunity for the number of people who choose to follow you will increase. And as the number of your Tweets increases, you will be found more often when searched, giving you more credibility as an expert in your area—and even more followers. Rome wasn't built in a day, and neither will the number of your followers.

Getting Started with Twitter

1. Register at *www.Twitter.com* hopefully, no one's taken your personal (or company) name yet.

2. Lurk: Follow others.

   - Follow your customers, the decision makers at those businesses, your suppliers, your competitors, industry gurus, regulators, etc.

   - Do a Twitter search on what you sell and on your industry, and click through to look at the posts. Decide whether the people who are posting the information are worthy of following.

   - Follow your employees. This is a great way to understand the buzz within your own company—and identify any inappropriate postings.

   - What you will find is that many people will return the favor of your follow, by following you back, allowing you to build your followership.

3. Choose your strategy: stay a lurker or choose something more active: an asker, strategic sender, or trusted guru. We recommend that you remain a lurker for at least a period of time, in order to develop a comfort level with the medium.

4. No matter what your chosen strategy, do some experimentation with the other modes. What's the worst that could happen if you asked the Twitterverse a question?

5. Once your list of followers (and those you follow) begins to grow, stay organized using HootSuite, Seesmic, or TweetDeck to manage the initiative.

> ### Advanced Tip
>
> *When there are multiple audiences, each with a different objective, set up multiple Twitter accounts: the more single-purpose the messages, the more attractive the Tweets will be to each audi-*

6. Often, an organization decides to start an initiative like Twitter by assigning one person to investigate and try different things. After a period of time, however, this responsibility should be split across different people and different departments. The marketing, HR, and sales departments will have different uses for Twitter; they should focus their attention on what they need to get from the tool.

7. Although you may think you are writing about what is important to you, it is critical to keep in mind what is important to your followers, and why they decided to follow you—otherwise they will "unfollow" you. The more single-topic-focused you can make it, the better the conversation will be. Chapter 15 contains dozens of ways to use Twitter; the key is to tie your initiative back to your objectives and audiences.

> **Time Saver**
>
> *For senior managers who have Twitter accounts, delegate the Twitter update responsibility; they don't need to do everything themselves.*

First Steps

1. Register, and follow the instructions in the previous section, "Getting Started with Twitter."

2. You may be surprised to find out that people within your company are already using Twitter on behalf of the organization. Find out what they're doing, and make sure they are in compliance with your company's policies and procedures. You will need to decide whether to recruit them to your "Twitter Team" or to shut them down completely. Policies and procedures should be communicated to your staff, so that they know what they can and cannot do using Twitter.

3. Do some competitive investigation: how are your competitors using the tool? Advanced Social Media marketers should think strategically and innovatively on how to use the Twitter platform to achieve their objectives; it's not just *"where are you?"* and *"what are you doing?"* any more.

Additional Resources

Here are some additional resources that you may find useful.

Software/Tools

- HootSuite, TweetDeck, Seesmic, Twellow, as seen throughout this chapter.

- Friend or Follow (*http://friendorfollow.com*)—Free
  Find out whether or not the people that you're following are following you back. You can also use this tool to see whether or not you're following the people that are following you.

- FollowCost (*http://followcost.com*)—Free
  Sometimes Twitter users seem to Tweet about a million times a day—taking over your Twitter feed and making it impossible to see the Tweets that you actually care about. FollowCost allows you to enter a username before you follow him or her to check out how often the user Tweets.

- My Cleenr (*http://www.mycleenr.com*)—Free
  This resource provides an easy way to see how active the accounts are that you follow. My Cleenr sorts the people that you follow based on their latest Tweet. You can easily see which accounts are outdated or are no longer used and unfollow those users.

- TwitHawk (*http://www.twithawk.com*)—Free trial (10 Tweets) and then fee-based
  TwitHawk allows you to monitor all of the Tweets on Twitter in order to catch when people are talking about your company or a service that you provide. Settings can be adjusted for customized search terms or geographic areas. For example, for a tourism attraction company, you may want to monitor Tweets mentioning "bored" or "what to do" in the city in which you're located. TwitHawk can automatically let you know about anyone in Branson, Missouri who is bored, and you can automatically Tweet back to him or her with a special discount on tickets today at your wax museum. You can also adjust the settings to automatically send a prewritten Tweet, or you can skim through the daily results in order to determine which you'd like to respond to.

- Twitterator (*http://www.twitterator.org*)—Free
  Have you ever seen one of those Web sites that lists "100 Social Media Experts to Follow on Twitter" or something to that effect? It's a pain to go through this list and click on each user individually, only to be taken to their Twitter page and have to click "Follow" for each person. This

tool allows you to copy and paste the URL, and the list of usernames will be followed in just one click.

- Just Tweet It (*http://justtweetit.com*)—Free
  Just Tweet It allows you to find other Twitter users that have similar interests to your own. Find people within your industry and list your Twitter account so that others can find you.

- TweetCall (*https://www.tweetcall.com*)—Free
  Do you have breaking news, or are you too busy to type out your Tweets? No access to a computer, BlackBerry, or iPhone? No problem—use this service to call in your Tweets. The toll-free number is a free service that transcribes your voice and posts to Twitter as text.

- TwitterHolic (*http://twitterholic.com*)—Free
  Use this Web site to see who the most popular users on Twitter are. The site lists the most popular users based on followers, and you can also check your own popularity rating.

- Qwitter (*http://useqwitter.com*)—Free
  Use this resource to find out who has stopped following you on Twitter. This can be helpful to determine which of your Tweets are turning followers away. You'll receive an email notification letting you know who stopped following you, and what your last Tweet was when they stopped.

- Susan and Randall are always updating their social bookmarks with great tools and resources. Check them out at Diigo:

  - Susan's are available at *www.diigo.com/user/susansweeney*.

  - Randall's are available at *www.diigo.com/user/RandallCraig*.

Education

- Susan has ongoing live webinars and recorded online courses on this topic available through the webinars and online store at her site, *http://www.susansweeney.com*, and provides access to others' courses on the subject through her online learning portal, eLearningU, at *http://www.elearningu.com*.

- Randall delivers workshops and webinars on this and related Social Media topics, all available at *www.RandallCraig.com.*

Articles

- Twitter 101 for Business (*http://business.twitter.com/twitter101*)

- 17 Ways You Can Use Twitter: A Guide for Beginners and Businesses (*http://www.doshdosh.com/ways-you-can-use-twitter*)

Books

- *Twitter Power: How to Dominate Your Market One Tweet at a Time*, by Joel Comm
  Understand how Twitter can help you reach your target market and increase your online presence. Develop marketing strategies and techniques to leverage your Twitter account and reach new markets. Also included in the book is a 30-day plan for dominating Twitter. A great book for those just getting started with Twitter.

- *The Twitter Book*, by Tim O'Reilly and Sarah Milstein
  Ideas, advice, and resources for building your brand on Twitter. The chapters are easy to understand and are written in full color to ensure an easy read. Understand how to search on Twitter, which programs to use to keep track of your Tweets, and the art of following. Like the 140-character limit on Twitter, this book is short and succinct, but filled with great information for those new to Twitter.

9

YouTube and Other Video-Sharing Sites

Overview

YouTube (*www.YouTube.com*) is a video-sharing Web site that is one of the most popular Web sites in the world. People are watching hundreds of millions of videos a day. According to YouTube, 20 hours of video is being uploaded to its site every hour—now, that's a lot of video!

Everyone is recording video these days, from their mobile phones, their webcams, and inexpensive high-definition recorders like the Flip, which has a USB connection enabling users to quickly and easily upload their video to YouTube.

YouTube has a number of features that make it great for businesses and the online marketer—things like:

- Video embedding. Once a user has uploaded a video to YouTube, the "embed" code can be copied to insert the video into his or her Web site or blog.

- Tagging. Users can develop their own titled description, and tags, enabling them to be found easily by their target market and the search engines.

Figure 9.1. With YouTube, you can have your own customized channel with its own Web address.

- Have your own channel. You can have your own channel (Figure 9.1), which makes it easy for subscribers to follow you and know when you have uploaded videos.

- Public or private videos. You get to choose whether you want specific videos to be available only to certain people (up to 25), or whether you want them to be available to the world.

- TestTube (Figure 9.2) enables users to take advantage of features as they are being developed and tested—things like the ability to add captions and annotations to your videos.

Creating Video Is Easy

Creating video is super easy these days. With a Flip video camera or virtually any digital recorder, you can take a video and upload it to YouTube in a matter of minutes. There is no fee for uploading or hosting your video.

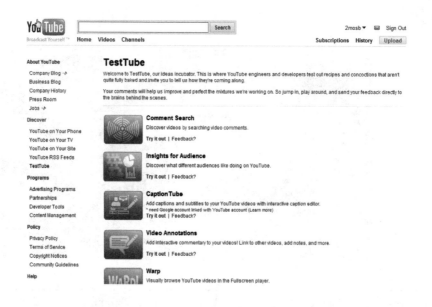

Figure 9.2. YouTube's TestTube area provides access to many applications that work with your YouTube videos.

There are many free and easy-to-use video editors available, such as Microsoft Movie Maker and Apple iMovie. Couple that with the free tools provided by YouTube through TestTube, such as Captions or Annotations, and you can have a first-rate marketing video online.

As with everything online, go back to your objectives, target market, and products and services to determine what to include. If you want the video to generate traffic, use the tools to overlay your Web address or have your "close" reference something viewers can get free from your Web site. If you want to sell more product, you might have third-party testimonials. If you want to cut down on customer service calls, you will have videos to provide the solution to common customer service problems.

You see all types of videos online. Home-made videos are the norm on YouTube. However, if you have professionally developed videos, they are certainly well received as well.

In regard to video length, generally shorter is better. You have many visitors with a short attention span. However, if your video provides them with the specific information they are looking for, they will stay until they get the needed information. The limits set by YouTube are 10 minutes in length and 2 GB in file size. They allow you to upload up to 10 videos at a time.

Figure 9.3. Tubemogul is a great video-syndication tool.

Sharing Is Easy

YouTube enables you to share your videos and other people's videos that you have added to your favorites through your profile on Facebook and Twitter. You simply connect your YouTube account to your Facebook and Twitter accounts through a very simple process.

You can also submit your video to video syndication sites like Tubemogul (*http://www.tubemogul.com*; see Figure 9.3). See more on video syndication at the end of this chapter.

Make Your Video Easy to Find

You've developed great videos; now you want to get as many of your target market as possible to view them. You want your videos to come up at the top of the search results within YouTube and also through the search engine results.

Before you start to determine titles, descriptions, and tags, you will want to review the keyword phrases you have focused on with your Web site or blog search engine optimization to see if there are any that fit with the content of the video. You will also want to look at what phrases your target market might choose when searching for a video like yours. You will want to have consistency with the keyword phrase you use in your title, in the description, and in the tags you use with each video. Be careful not to waste tag space on irrelevant words.

At this point you will also decide the appropriate category for your video. You need the correct category or your video will not be found. The smaller the category, the less competition and the easier it will be for you to rank high in a search.

Getting on the YouTube Home Page

The home page of YouTube is visited by millions of people daily. If you can get your video there, your video will receive significant views. How does a video get this placement? YouTube has its own algorithm that determines which video receives the honor. Although YouTube does not provide the algorithm details, it has been speculated that it is impacted by:

- The number of friends you have

- The number of subscribers you have

- The number of channel views you have

- The number of comments on your video

- The rating of your video

- The number of times your video has become a "favorite"

- The number of views in a day

- The category you submit to and the type of channel you created has a lot to do with success in getting honors. Gurus tend to get honors pretty easily.

Create and Customize Your Own Channel

YouTube makes it easy for you to have your own channel. There are a number of benefits to having your own channel, including:

- You have all your videos in one place and easily accessible to your target market. You can choose to also include other people's videos in your channel.

- You get to have your own YouTube URL. You get to choose the name. The name you choose should reinforce your brand or relate to your important keywords, or both if possible. Your URL will look like this: *http://www.youtube.com/yournamehere* (e.g., *http://www.youtube.com/rmcraig* for one of Randall's channels).

- When you have your own channel, you get to set up your own profile, which can be keyword rich and also link back to your site or blog. Make the link anchor text be your important keywords to help with SEO.

- You can customize your channel.

Channel Customization

It is easy to customize your channel on YouTube. You can create an impression, make a statement, and keep your viewers engaged with your customization.

To customize your channel, you simply log into your YouTube account and click the yellow "*Edit Channel*" button. Then you can set up your channel details such as your Web site URL, channel description, about you, profile picture, etc. You can also choose your theme from a number of themes provided or you can upload a custom background image. You can choose the colors for background, links, and border. You can choose to display uploaded videos, favorites, playlists, or a combination of all three.

If you choose to display your playlists, you can then select the individual video playlists you want to include. You will have the option to edit the featured content set and the featured video for your channel. The featured video is the one your channel visitors will see first, so make sure you choose the right setting.

From the Channel page you can edit: subscribers, friends, and channel comments; you also can edit profile information as well as channel settings, themes, and modules.

You can also click through on the Modules tab to remove or display content modules: comments, recent activity, friends, subscribers, groups, and subscriptions.

Promote Your Channel and Your Videos

You will want to have a strategy to promote your channel and your videos. In an ideal world you would have a plan for your video to go viral, but this is difficult to do. It is difficult to predict what will make a video take on a life of its own; there is no guarantee . . . sometimes you just happen to hit a home run. Videos that do go viral sometimes involve controversy—perhaps when the "little guy" takes a stand like United Breaks Guitars enjoyed 6,568,707 views in five months. (The musician Dave Carroll and The Sons of Maxwell are from Susan Sweeney's hometown—what a small world!) Sometimes the video goes viral because it is cute or heartwarming, like the Otters Holding Hands video from the Vancouver Aquarium which saw 13,375,724 views in two years. Still other videos go viral because of their unique content, like the What Will Blend Channel that has 92 videos in the series and 217,720 subscribers who want to see what the team at Blendtec will try to put through the blender next.

Ways to promote your channel and your videos include:

- Use the share option. You can share by email address or through a number of Social Media venues.

- Invite friends, fans, and followers in your Social Media venues to subscribe to your channel.

- Promote your channel in your outbound marketing—in your ezine or newsletter.

- Put a link to your channel on your Web site or your blog (Figure 9.4).

- Put a link to your channel on your Facebook, Twitter, and LinkedIn profiles.

- Add your channel link to your signature file.

- Leave comments on popular videos in your niche. Get your comment in early so it appears at the top.

- Use the *"Find Your Friends"* feature in YouTube.

Figure 9.4. Provide access to your YouTube channel from your Web site.

Join or Create YouTube Groups

Like most of the other Social Media sites, YouTube also has groups where users share and discuss videos. You can join an existing group and participate or you can create your own group.

Advertise on YouTube

YouTube has both self-managed advertising and accounts that are managed by Google sales representatives. The advertising can be purchased through YouTube or Google AdWords. Details on YouTube advertising options can be found at *http://www.youtube.com/t/advertising*.

Other Opportunities and Options with YouTube

- **YouTube Streams.** With YouTube Streams you can share YouTube with other people in real time. With Streams, you can create your own You-Tube room to watch and interact with other users while sharing videos, or you can join someone else's stream. Participants can add videos from their Favorites, from their QuickList, or they can provide links to videos. They can also make a running commentary as the videos play.

- **Active Sharing.** With Active Sharing you can broadcast the videos you are watching. If you choose to turn on Active Sharing, your username will appear next to every video you visit for 30 minutes.

Video Syndication

One of the more exciting developments in the world of internet video is the movement to **syndication**. In the olden days of 2008, if you wanted your video to be hosted on several of the video-sharing sites, you had to manually upload each of your videos to each of the services. Not only was this time-consuming, but to aggregate the analytics or earn money through advertising was just about impossible.

Syndication

The supply of material for reuse and integration with other material.

To solve this problem, a number of video sites started making partnership deals: in exchange for sending (e.g., syndicating) a user's videos, they (and the video owners) would share in any advertising revenue.

Consider this example, taken from Randall Craig's Professionally Speaking TV (Figure 9.5) weekly interview show. The Web site for the show itself is *www. ProfessionallySpeakingTV.com*. The video is hosted elsewhere—on one of the video hosting/syndication sites, in this case blip.tv. If you go to http://prospeaking. blip.tv, you will see all of the episodes, hosted on the native platform. Whenever a new episode is uploaded, it is distributed to about a dozen other video sites— all with their own audiences. As an example, you are able to watch episodes of Professionally Speaking TV in iTunes; just search the iTunes store for "Randall Craig" and it should come up. (One of the interviews is between Randall Craig and Susan Sweeney.) All of the viewership statistics are flowed back to blip.tv, where they are aggregated and made available for viewing.

First Steps

1. If you don't currently use YouTube, spend some time getting familiar with it. A great way to do this is to search YouTube for your products and company name.

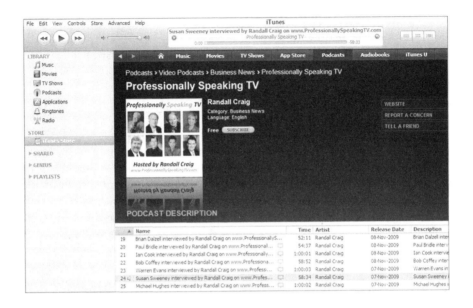

Figure 9.5. Through syndication, Randall's Professionally Speaking TV videos are accessible on a number of sites, including iTunes.

2. Register on YouTube to capture your company name and the names of your major brands. Whether you choose to do anything on the platform or not is a decision you will make later.

3. Inventory all of the existing video assets you might have that could be repurposed onto YouTube.

4. For advanced Social Media marketers, now is the time to tie your YouTube participation back to your objectives. This might mean Social Media SEO, putting text overlays with your Web address on each video to drive traffic back to your site, incorporating calls to action, etc.

5. Again for the advanced Social Media marketer, explore how video syndication can be used to drive even more video views.

Additional Resources

Here are some additional resources that you may find useful.

Software/Tools

- Splicd (*http://www.splicd.com*)—Free
  This tool allows you to send out a link that starts your video at a particular time point. Perhaps you have a ten-minute video describing a number of the products you offer, but you're sending out a link related to only one of those products. Splicd gives you the opportunity to provide a link start at, say, 5:17 into the video, so that the viewers see the clip you're intending for them to see.

- YouTube Badge (*http://flashandburn.net/youtubeBadge*)—Free
  This tool creates a YouTube badge that you can post to your Web site, blog, or Facebook page to show visitors the six latest videos you've posted to YouTube.

- CaptionTube (*http://captiontube.appspot.com*)—Free
  CaptionTube allows you to create and apply captions to your YouTube videos. Captions can also be used as a transcript for viewers to read.

- Jay Cut (*http://jaycut.com*)—Free
  This is an online video-editing tool. Use Jay Cut to edit out different parts of a clip, compile multiple clips into one video, add captions and music, or make your own slideshow—all from your browser. Videos are then ready to upload to video sites like YouTube.

- One True Media (*http://www.onetruemedia.com/otm_site/public_ home*)—Free
  Mix your photos and video clips to create a video collage. Add captions, transitions, special effects, and music to enhance your video. Created videos can then be shared online or burned to DVD.

- Susan and Randall are always updating their social bookmarks with great tools and resources. Check them out at Diigo:

  - Susan's are available at *www.diigo.com/user/susansweeney.*

    – Randall's are available at *www.diigo.com/user/RandallCraig.*

Education

- Susan has ongoing live webinars and recorded online courses on this topic available through the webinars and online store at her site, *http://www.susansweeney.com,* and provides access to others' courses on the subject through her online learning portal, eLearningU, at *http://www.elearningu.com.*

- Randall delivers workshops and webinars on this and related Social Media topics, all available at *www.RandallCraig.com.*

Books

- *YouTube: An Insider's Guide to Climbing the Charts*, by Alan Lastufka and Michael W. Dean
  Written by two YouTube experts with millions of views; learn how to make, optimize, encode, upload, and promote a high-quality video. The book covers topics such as equipment to use, editing, and a 99-cent film school chapter on how to film a video.

- *YouTube and Video Marketing: An Hour a Day*, by Greg Jarboe and Suzie Reider
  This book offers step-by-step instructions on how to succeed with YouTube. Topics include YouTube channels, video-production tips, search engine optimization for your YouTube videos, and how to track, measure, and analyze your video marketing efforts.

10

MySpace

MySpace (*www.myspace.com*) is currently in very tight competition with Facebook as the preeminent consumer-based Social Media platform. While the jury is out as to who will win the war, on the basis of sheer numbers of active users, it looks like the edge is going to Facebook.

Notwithstanding this trend, users are fickle, and with over 125 million active monthly users around the globe (about half in the United States), MySpace is still a potent force. In particular, it has developed exceptionally strong niches in several areas, particularly in entertainment (e.g., musicians, celebrities, comedians). Because of the numbers involved, ignoring MySpace as a platform is almost foolhardy, particularly for consumer-oriented businesses.

Profile Page

Every user has a MySpace page, which they can customize with different modules. This page is shown when they log on and is the primary way a user begins interacting with others. Again, like Facebook, people who have accepted your invitations are called "*friends*," and for the most part, friends are able to see what you have posted within MySpace. Profiles are generally designed for individuals, although it is possible to create a page for your organization. (MySpace prefers that you create an organization page as a "Brand Community," which is described later in this chapter.)

Profile Page Customization

If you are looking to create a profile, one of the first things you will want to do is to customize it, by adding—or removing—the appropriate modules . Here is a list of some of the more likely ones that you may want to have appear:

- Activity stream—shows what each of your friends are doing.

- Comments—shows any comments from you or your friends.

- Companies—notes what is shown within the Companies area of your profile.

- Friend space—identifies your friends (either Top, Random, Who's Online, or Recent).

- Groups—shows which groups you belong to.

- RSS reader—allows you to funnel in an external-to-MySpace blog (Figure 10.1). (More on blogs later in the chapter.)

- Video player—allows you to play uploaded videos.

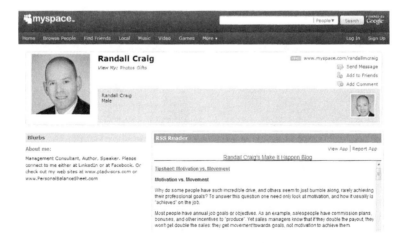

Figure 10.1. Randall's blog posts are accessible through RSS on many sites, including his MySpace profile.

Of course, you will want to upload a photo and add some other personal details. Be careful about adding any details that you don't want shared publicly. Even with MySpace's built-in privacy controls, it is too easy for your information to appear—or be shared—openly.

Groups

There are literally millions of groups (Figure 10.2) that exist on MySpace, under just about every category. Each group has its own page, as well as discussion forum, bulletins, friends lists, etc. The group creator can choose whether the group is public or private, whether it is hidden or not, and even whether members can invite others or not.

The challenge with these groups is that there is very little ability to custom-brand the pages, and compared to brand communities, groups are like the Wild West: Many groups are replete with spam comments—"advertising" for nonrelated products.

For this last reason more than most, participation within others' groups should be done mindfully. Adding perspective, user help, and links to resources in response to a question are all acceptable. Asking users questions in order to test-drive a new idea, or asking for their suggestions, is also acceptable. Blatant product pitches will likely harm your brand more than help, and should be avoided.

Figure 10.2.   MySpace has a great search feature to enable you to find the perfect group for your purposes.

One possible idea for a group is your company's alumni. If you hire people who are in a young demographic, starting a group as a way to maintain your connection to them might make sense. It is most unlikely that the younger demographic will be on LinkedIn.

Forums

There are well-trafficked discussion groups on just about every topic within the MySpace forums. These forums are separate and distinct from the discussion forums contained within MySpace groups. There are rules that limit commercial postings on the forums, but the postings still can be found from time to time.

As is the case with participation within MySpace group forums (or any internet discussion group), the nature of your participation should be strategic, not commercial. MySpace forum participation is appropriate only if your target demographic spends time there—otherwise, skip it.

Advanced Tip

Groups have very limited moderation capabilities; it is very easy for inappropriate content to be posted, so a scheduled review and deletion of posts is critical. Consider a warning within the group description that states that any off-topic or commercial postings will be deleted and the member who posted them will be banned.

Events

MySpace has the ability to create events. The events can be found by anyone within MySpace by searching, and by direct invitation to your friends. The event can be a "live" event at a physical address, or it can be an online event.

For the most part, MySpace events are used by bands to introduce a new album, the location for a gig, school reunions, and (seemingly) smaller events. It doesn't appear to be used by many others. This doesn't mean that there isn't an opportunity: If you have a large number of MySpace friends, or you are targeting a younger demographic, then using the Events functionality is a convenient way to spread the message.

Note: Events are used far more in the United States than in other MySpace countries. If you are hoping to build an event elsewhere, MySpace (and MySpace Events) may not be the most effective tool.

Applications

There are hundreds of applications that have been written for MySpace: games, religion-inspired, utilities, video players, etc. If you think you might want something in particular, simply search MySpace applications to find it.

An example: You want to have your Twitter updates appear within your MySpace profile. Searching for Twitter within MySpace shows eight applications. One of them, iTwitter, does exactly what you want and has over 270,000 users—more than any of the other seven. At the same time, you notice that another application, Twitter Sync (with over 23,000 users) can automatically synchronize your Twitter posting and your MySpace status. Hmmm.

From a company standpoint, there is another potential opportunity with applications: to write your own. If the application is downloaded and used, then your message can be broadcast not just to the users, but virally, to all of the users' friends.

An example: If you were a food manufacturer, you might create an application that allowed the sharing of recipes. As each person entered recipes, he or she would see your branding. And then as the users sent their recipes to their friends, they also would see your branding. If they chose to participate by posting their recipes in turn, then your branding would be distributed even farther.

One of the challenges of developing your own application (beyond the cost of development and the cost of promoting the application within MySpace) is that a greater number of people are using Social Media on their mobile devices. MySpace, for example, has a free app for iPhones that provides access to status, the activity stream, and a few other basic functions—but no capability to run the MySpace application that you've developed for the Web. Ditto for BlackBerry, iPhone, and Android.

Blogs

MySpace has built-in the functionality to give each of its users his or her own blog. Our recommendation for any company that wants a blog is to build it into their Web site directly, or if this is not possible, to host it themselves and link to it from their main Web site. In order to get your company blog funneled in to any MySpace page, you will need to add the RSS Reader. The unfortunately named "My Blog" refers to the MySpace-created blog, not your external company blog.

Email and Instant Messaging

One of the major problems with standard email is spam. The benefit of the MySpace email system is that any email message sent within the system has a known sender. It is impossible for a sender to hide behind the veil of anonymity. And because the system is designed for consumers, it is impossible to send "bulk" junk mail to everyone. It is also impossible for a person to send a message from the outside internet directly to a MySpace email address.

Interestingly, many teenagers rarely check their standard email, relying completely on their Social Media email addresses to communicate. This is troubling for marketers who see the creation of an email list as their primary marketing goal. On the other hand, it also speaks to opportunity for those who understand Social Media marketing: People trust recommendations from their friends and are interested in engaging in meaningful conversation.

MySpace also has a built-in ability to instant-message any of your friends who are online at the same time you are. While there is little corporate value in this functionality, it also speaks to the importance of the social network and how easy it can be for people to connect.

Advertising

Like almost every other Social Media site, MySpace includes the ability to advertise. Upon registration, every user must include some demographic details. This information, combined with information displayed in your profile, allows MySpace to target advertising to you.

Annoyingly, advertising for MySpace is done on a country-by-country basis. In the United States, for example, targeting can be done on the following factors, on a self-serve basis:

- Gender

- Age (or age range)

- Education

- Relationship. This includes nonstandard categories such as recently engaged, recently married, recent breakup, etc.

- Parental status. Once again, some unique categories, including the age of the children, just gave birth, expecting, etc.

- Location. The ability to target advertising can be done on a regional, state/city, or radius from a zip code.

- Interests and occupations. This tool provides an incredibly robust number of selection criteria. As an example, to select users whose interest is in books, there are further subcatagories based on interests in specific authors and titles. To select users whose interests are related to sports, there are further choices down to specific team names and certain sports celebrities.

In Canada and the United Kingdom, advertising is handled by contacting MySpace directly in that country, although they do post some basic information on the "packages" online. In most international markets, a direct inquiry is necessary to even start the process.

Advanced Tip

No matter which you use (PPC or CPM), you specify the destination Web page for when the user clicks the advertisement. Instead of routing them to your Web site's home page, create a special landing page with special messaging for the MySpace user, with specifics of your offer.

Also, instead of creating just one advertisement, create a family of them, with slightly different titles and text. Then monitor the click-through rates, dropping the less-effective ones. The marketing term for this is called split-testing, or A-B testing. If you're really keen, take the successful advertisements and route the user to different landing pages; you can do split testing on the effectiveness of your own Web site as well.

Advertising is easy, and it creates awareness, but it certainly isn't conversation, and it's about as far from the goal of Social Media as it could be. But a relevant call to action in an advertisement still might be the first step toward a transaction.

Advertising is sold on both a pay-per-click (PPC) and a pay-per-impression (CPM) basis. There are several reasons that you might prefer one over the other:

- **Pay-per-click:** By choosing this method, there is no charge for displaying your advertisement, but every time a person clicks it, you are charged a fee. When ordering a PPC advertisement, you set a maximum daily (or ad lifetime) budget, as well as a bid price for the ad itself. Depending on how much others bid, your advertisement will be shown more, or less. By monitoring the advertising statistics, you can increase (or decrease) your bid, which will then increase (or decrease) how often your ad is displayed.

One of the advantages of PPC advertising is that the cost is incurred only when a person clicks through, which makes it far easier to directly calculate the cost of prospect acquisition. (Of course, the full cost of client acquisition also hinges on your Web site's ability to convert that prospect into a real client.)

PPC bids are usually in the four- to ten-cent range.

- **Pay-per-impression:** CPM advertising is more appropriate if you want to ensure that your advertising is actually seen by a certain number of people. Like with PPC, MySpace uses a bidding system to determine how often your ad appears. The higher your CPM bid, the more frequently your advertisement will run, and the faster you will generate awareness with your target audience.

  CPM bids might be found in the six- to twenty-five-cent range per 1,000 impressions.

MySpace Brand Communities

A far more powerful way to interact with audiences is to create a MySpace brand community. (This is similar to a Facebook fan page.) It may contain any number of special-purpose applications that can increase engagement, as well as uploaded photos, videos, and other content.

MySpace has two different types of brand communities: self-serve and full-serve. Self-serve requires a solid knowledge of HTML and has limited functionality. Full-serve provides more functionality, as well as monitoring, but requires an investment in advertising.

Here are examples of some of the special capabilities in the full-serve model:

- **Content monitoring:** MySpace will review your community twice daily and delete inappropriate content. The criteria for inappropriate content would be defined by you.

- **Sweepstakes:** A random winner is chosen from the brand community's friends.

- **User-generated content:** Friends can upload a particular type of content (text, photo, mp3, etc.). This might be useful for contests, compilations of stories, etc.

- **Quiz:** This can be a multiple-choice quiz with up to 15 questions. The quiz can be used to qualify contestants for a contest, to collect market research, or any other purpose.

- **Auto-commenter:** This will automatically submit comments to friends either when they join or when they add a comment on the Brand Community page.

Probably the most powerful use of brand communities is their value as a source for market research. Putting aside issues of self-selection bias (e.g., that users self-register and therefore bias any market research results), brand community members can be used as a highly motivated focus group. The conversational nature of Social Media makes it easy to collect ad hoc feedback and ask open-ended questions. In addition, the "*MyInsights*" tool provides a window to users' demographics.

Overall Recommendation

Unless you have evidence that your customers or prospects spend time on MySpace, we would recommend caution before investing significantly. Furthermore, the platform is facing a war of attrition as its users slowly defect to other Social Media sites, primarily Facebook. Nevertheless, there is still a critical mass of well-connected users, and if the demographic is right, MySpace is too big to ignore.

First Steps

1. Explore MySpace forums and groups to determine whether or not your customers can be found there.

2. Search for your competitors to learn more about their Social Media strategy.

3. Register your company name and brands as users to prevent others from taking them; this should be done with all the Social Media sites.

Additional Resources

Here are some additional resources that you may find useful.

Software/Tools

- MySpace Gateway (*www.myspacegateway.com*)
  This one site has links to hundreds of other "add-on" sites and resources that allow you to change the layout, add functionality, or otherwise personalize your MySpace page. The site is replete with advertising that looks like real content, so make sure you know what you're clicking before you do so.

- MySpace Compilation (*www.myspace-compilation.com*)
  This site is very similar to the Gateway resource, but a bit easier to understand. It requires a strong understanding of MySpace layouts; suitable for your Webmaster.

- MySpace's help page (*http://faq.myspace.com*)
  This site is helpful, with the top MySpace questions, searches, and a listing of the current MySpace issues, straight from the source!

- Susan and Randall are always updating their social bookmarks with great tools and resources. Check them out at Diigo:

  - Susan's are available at *www.diigo.com/user/susansweeney.*

  - Randall's are available at *www.diigo.com/user/RandallCraig.*

Articles

- "eHow: MySpace" (*http://www.ehow.com/articles_4506-myspace.html*)
  This answers site has some 800+ articles on how to do just about everything on MySpace. Narrow this list down by using the navigation on the side of the page or by using the site's *search* functionality.

11

Flickr

Flickr (Figure 11.1) is a social photography site that enables the user to upload, edit, manage, and share photographs with friends, family, other Flickr users, and the internet at large. Flickr hosts your photos on its server, saving you bandwidth and acting as an additional backup for your images.

Figure 11.1. Flickr is one of the most popular photo-hosting sites, with many features and functionality.

Flickr has been integrated with Yahoo! Image Search, meaning that pictures from Flickr will be displayed when a search for images is done on Yahoo! Photos on Flickr are also indexed by Google and Technorati, showing up in their search results. If one of your pictures shows up in a person's search results, they are directed to your individual photo pages where they are made aware of you . . . and can then be directed to your Web site or blog.

Flickr is owned by Yahoo!, so you will need a Yahoo! ID to sign up.

You should be aware of and abide by Flickr's Terms of Use: "Flickr is for personal use only. If we find you selling products, services, or yourself through your photostream, we will terminate your account." You also cannot "upload, post, email, transmit or otherwise make available any unsolicited or unauthorized advertising, promotional materials, 'junk mail,' 'spam,' 'chain letters,' 'pyramid schemes,' or any other form of illegal solicitation. You may, however, make legally compliant solicitations in those areas (such as shopping rooms) that are designated for such purpose."

Sign Up for an Account

First you need to sign up for an account. You can have a free account or you can pay to have a Pro account. What's the difference?

With a free account you get:

- Two video uploads each month

- Maximum 90 seconds

- Maximum 150 MB file

- Up to 100 MB of photographs each month

- Maximum 10 MB per photo

- Photostream views limited to the 200 most recent images

- Photos posted in up to 10 group pools

- Ads are displayed as you browse and share.

The Pro account costs $24.95 a year, and you get:

- Unlimited photo uploads

- Maximum 20 MB per photo

- Unlimited video uploads

  - Maximum 90 seconds

  - Maximum 500 MB per video

- The ability to show high-definition video

  - Unlimited storage

  - Unlimited bandwidth

- Posting of photos or videos in up to 60 group pools

- Ad-free browsing and sharing

- View count and referrer statistics.

Once you have set up your account, you log in and edit your settings and develop your profile. You should:

- Upload a buddy icon. This can be your favorite image, your logo, or some other appealing graphic.

- Set your screen name. This can be your Web address, your brand, or your name. If you use your Web address as your screen name, it will be attached to every photo you upload and every message you post in Flickr groups.

- Build your profile. Tell visitors about you, your business, and your brand. You can include links. HTML is acceptable, so be sure to include your best keywords as anchor text when providing a link to your Web site or your blog.

- Create your Flickr Web address. This makes it easy to share your photos and videos with the world. Make your address something that is easy for your target market to remember. Your Flickr address will be something like *http://www.flickr.com/photos/yourname.*

Upload Photos and Videos

Once you have an account, you can upload your photos and videos. This can be done from your desktop, through email, or from your cameraphone. Flickr has a great Web interface where you can upload your photos, or you can use their upload tool (called Flickr Uploadr) where you can drag and drop your photos from your desktop to Uploadr. You can also upload via email, through iPhoto, Aperture, or through several third-party desktop programs. On your phone you can take a picture or video and email it to Flickr.

When you upload, you are able to add a title, description, and tags, which are all very important for your being found on Flickr by other Flickr users, but also important for being found through Yahoo!, Google, and Technorati.

Note that Flickr allows only very short videos to be uploaded. Longer videos need to appear within YouTube or a similar video-sharing site. For ease of management, we recommend that you keep your videos in one place, not several.

Have a strategy for search optimization. Review your most important keyword phrases. Review the terms that your target market is likely going to search on when they are looking for your products and services. You will want to have consistency for the term in your title, description, and tags. You can have up to 75 tags per photo.

Tags are like keywords that help users find your photo. There are various ways that people tag photos:

- Profession

- Names of individuals in the picture

- Location—useful for tourism and geographic-specific businesses

- Medium—photo, video, illustration

- Type—candid, photo shoot, magazine shoot

- Brand—Mercedes, Flip

- Relevant publications—Coastal Living, Vogue

- Your Web site.

With the title and description you have fewer characters. Think about your keywords and also your brand in the title, and maybe even your Web address. In the description, HTML is allowed, so think about having a link to your Web site or blog with your most important keywords as the anchor text. Also think about the destination URL being a landing page rather than your home page.

You can edit your photos within Flickr through their partner, Picnik. You can remove red eyes, rotate, resize, crop, sharpen images, etc.

Organize Your Photos and Videos

Flickr has an Organizr feature that enables you to organize your photos into sets and collections. Organizr also enables you to perform common tasks on large batches of photos and videos, such as tagging, changing permissions, or editing timestamps.

You organize your photos into sets and collections. Sets are like albums or groups of photos that relate to a common theme. It could be an event, a product, a location, or anything else that makes sense with your particular photos. Collections are groups of the albums or sets and might relate to the year they were taken, the location, or some other relationship for your sets.

Promote Your Photos and Videos

Now you are ready to share your photos and videos with the world. There are many ways to make that happen:

- Flickr users can find your content through the Flickr search feature. Your photos and videos will appear if your title, description, and tags relate to the keywords in the search.

- Yahoo!, Google, and Technorati users can access your images. Again, your photos and videos will appear if your title, description, and tags relate to the keywords in the search.

- Join groups that relate to your photo content, your business, and your target market. Once you join you can submit your pictures.

- Comment on others' pictures. This may get them or other users to click through to your profile page to view your pictures or to learn more about you.

- You can start your own group.

- Display your Flickr photos on your Web site or blog. (More on this "latr.")

- Provide a link from your Web site or blog to your Flickr pictures.

- Get your photo listed in Flickr's *"Explore,"* which is a daily collection of Flickr's most interesting photos.

- Invite your friends to join Flickr.

- Link to your photos from Facebook, LinkedIn, Twitter, and other Social Media venues.

Display Your Flickr Photos on Your Site or Blog

You can display your Flickr photos on your site by embedding a Flickr photo stream on your Web site or blog. Flickr has a wizard to enable you to set up a dynamic badge, or "widget," of your publicly viewable Flickr photos. With the wizard you choose your display options—which photos you want to display, the size, etc. You also specify if you want to display your screen name and buddy icon. Next you choose either a styled version of the badge (photos appear in a column with a colored background) or one that you can design yourself.

The site pictured in Figure 11.2, *www.elearningu.com*, shows a photostream from Flickr as part of a news entry. When someone clicks on the Flickr icon, he or she gets access to all the photos (see Figure 11.3). There are many third-party Flickr applications that allow you to display your Flickr photos in a range of different formats.

To display your Flickr pictures on your blog, there are many blog plug-ins available. Wordpress, for example, has both a Flickr Photo Album plug-in and a Flickr RSS plug-in.

Share Flickr Photos

Actively promote and approve the reuse of your photos that help to provide exposure to your products and services. Approve the requests to use your photos quickly—journalists often are on tight deadlines and you'd hate to lose out on having a great photo of your product or your destination included in a publica-

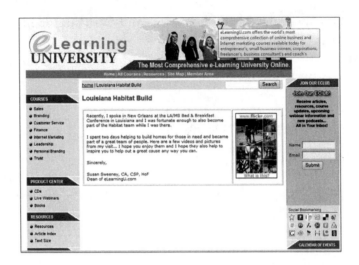

Figure 11.2.   Flickr provides the capability to incorporate your photos on your Web site.

Figure 11.3.   Flickr enables you to show your photos in a number of different ways on your site.

tion that is read by your target market just because you didn't respond quickly enough to a reuse request.

Enable Stats

Flickr has great tools for statistics, but you have to ask for them to be turned on. The stats include overall views, engagement, and referrals.

Flickr App Garden

Like Facebook, MySpace, LinkedIn, and just about every other Social Media platform, Flickr has recognized that allowing others to build more functionality adds value to the Flickr platform itself. Flickr calls its system an "App Garden." There are iPhone apps, geotagging apps, Twitter apps, etc. New applications are being added everyday. Check it out to see if there are applications you can use to help promote your photos.

First Steps

1. Begin inventorying your photos for possible inclusion onto Flickr.

2. Search for your company name, brands, and products, to understand any trends or grassroots buzz that you can latch on to.

3. Incorporate a Flickr photostream onto your Web site or blog, if appropriate.

Additional Resources

Here are some additional resources that you may find useful.

Software/Tools

- Big Huge Labs Flickr Toys (*http://bighugelabs.com*)
  This site lists dozens of toys, games, and utilities that allow you to do more with your Flickr photos: custom calendars and cards, posters, puzzles, movie posters, and more.

- Flickrstorm (*http://www.zoo-m.com/flickr-storm*)
  This is a neat search engine for Flickr that brings up additional related images.

- Tag Galaxy (*taggalaxy.de*)
  This is a powerful tool to visually discover photos based on their tags.

- 100+ Flickr Resources (*http://traffikd.com/resources/flickr*)
  This list, from a blog, is a wonderful listing of just about every Flickr plug-in available. Read through the page comments for even more links.

- Susan and Randall are always updating their social bookmarks with great tools and resources. Check them out at Diigo:

  - Susan's are available at *www.diigo.com/user/susansweeney*.

  - Randall's are available at *www.diigo.com/user/RandallCraig*.

Education

- Susan has ongoing live webinars and recorded online courses on this topic available through the webinars and online store at her site, *http://www.susansweeney.com*, and provides access to others' courses on the subject through her online learning portal, eLearningU, at *http://www.elearningu.com*.

12

Tier Two Sites

Overview

There is no question that there is a pecking order with Social Media sites. At the top of the list are YouTube, Facebook, LinkedIn, Twitter, Flickr, and MySpace. A second group—including about 300 sites—fits into a second tier because they are not as popular or, in the case of social bookmarking sites, have a specific purpose. As a reference point, Facebook has over 300 million account holders, while MySpace has 125 million, LinkedIn has 50 million, and Plaxo has about 20 million.

In this chapter and the next one, we describe some of the more well-traveled Tier Two sites and how you might take advantage of them—or not. We've tried to point out some of the distinguishing features, but you will note that many of the sites are in the "me too" category and, in the long run, may not survive unless they find a way to differentiate themselves. (Some differentiate themselves by geography, others by target demographic, others by the nature of their functionality and partnerships.)

Figure 12.1 is a partial list: how many have you heard of? (And how many do you think will still be around in five years?)

Blog or Information-oriented	Boomarking	Communication	Photo & Video
Alltop	Amplify	Bebo	Blip
Bigcontact	Blinklist	BlackPlanet	Dailybooth
Blogcatalog	Blogmarks.net	Brightkite	Dailymotion
Blogger	Clipmarks	eHow	Livevideo
Disqus	Del.icio.us	Friendster	Metacafe
Friendfeed	Diigo	Grou.ps	Picasa
Glogster	Faves	HubPages	SmugMug
Identi.ca	Gravee	Instructables	Ustream.tv
Lifeblog	Kirtsy	Massify	Viddler
Livejournal	Mixx	Netlog	Vimeo
Newsvine	Mylinkvault	Ning	
Posterous	Searchles	Slideshare	
Reddit	Simply	SocialGo	
Scribd	Squidoo	Socialight	
Tribe	Stumbleupon	Steam	
Tumblr	Tagfoot		
TypePad			
Wikipedia			
WordPress			

Figure 12.1.   Examples of Tier Two sites.

Just because all of these sites exist doesn't mean that you should have a presence on all of them. Here are several tests that you can use to determine which, if any, of these second-tier sites you might wish to invest your time and budget in:

- Whenever you do any formal market research, ask the respondents which Social Media sites they use. There is no sense fishing in a pond without fish.

- Whenever you have informal conversations with customers, prospects, suppliers, and recruits, ask them which Social Media sites they typically use, and which ones they have plans to use in the future.

- Do a simple search on your competitors' company names, and your product names on a number of these sites.

Plaxo

Plaxo (*www.plaxo.com*) (Figure 12.2) started a number of years ago as a system to keep your contact list up to date. You uploaded your contact list

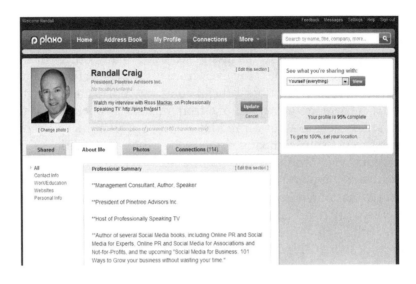

Figure 12.2. Plaxo is an online address book and Social Networking service, similar to LinkedIn.

to Plaxo, and each month the system would send an email to your list asking them to confirm their contact details. Many recipients who received the update request decided to use the system themselves, resulting in viral growth of the system as a whole.

The only problem was that the automated unsolicited update requests began to get annoying and were soon being disregarded or, worse, were regarded as spam.

The second phase of Plaxo's growth saw it de-emphasize (and eventually turn off) the address update service and implement a LinkedIn-style Social Networking site, centered on an online resume and connections.

Plaxo is currently emphasizing the feature they call "Plaxo Pulse"—a stream of status updates from Plaxo connections, Facebook, Twitter, and a number of other sites. When you go to *www.Plaxo.com*, the default home page is the Pulse page. It appears that they are making a play to be an aggregator; they aren't tapping ad revenues (except for Google ads), and they are not selling upgraded company pages. In fact, they haven't even yet embedded the company page concept into the system, except as a page that collects the Plaxo members who may have a company name within their profile. For this reason, Plaxo has limited utility at the company level.

On the other hand, it is a very useful site to perform due diligence on prospective customers, research the backgrounds of the employees at suppliers, etc. And like all the Social Media sites, many of your employees—and former employees—will use your company name within their profiles, impacting your company brand.

It may be tempting to dismiss Plaxo—and many others of these Tier Two sites—as not worthwhile. However, from a PR perspective it is useful to make sure that there is at least one official company representative with a profile on the site. If there are any questions from media, it is better that they contact a more senior person—not a random employee (or former employee) who just happens to list your company name in the profile. In addition, there is the SEO argument: Every profile that contains a link back to the company Web site will improve the company's Web site search engine ranking.

Plaxo was purchased a few years ago by the cable giant Comcast; as a result, it is safe to say that Plaxo is unlikely to fold for lack of financing. On the other hand, with a big corporate owner, the pace of innovation seems to be slower than its primary competitor, LinkedIn.

- **Registration:** As is expected, signing up on Plaxo is as simple as going to the home page and filling out a form. Even if you care very little about actually using Plaxo, register anyway, just to prevent someone from taking your name.

- **Social Media feeds:** If you wish to have your blog postings, photos, tweets, and other Social Media content automatically appearing within your profile, click on the *"About Me"* tab in your profile, select *"Web site,"* and then edit this section. There are over 40 Web sites that Plaxo can extract content from and publish on your profile or Plaxo Pulse page.

- **Job postings:** Plaxo has outsourced the job postings functionality to a separate company, SimplyHired.com, and their jobamatic offering. While quite rudimentary, this system will provide exposure to your job posting throughout the Plaxo site, through your connections, and potentially on other SimplyHired partner sites. Depending on whether your potential recruitment pool is on Plaxo or not, this can be incredibly cost-effective... or a complete waste of time.

- **Groups:** Like Facebook and LinkedIn, Plaxo has the capability for groups to be created for any purpose. The challenge is that the functionality is not fully mature; merely finding a listing of groups is tortuous at best. Skip it.

- **Fan pages:** Unlike Facebook fan pages, these really are fan pages—as in discussion groups for fans of different television shows. Needless to say, this consumer-focused add-in was the result of the Comcast purchase, and it is a bizarre dilution of Plaxo's business-oriented earlier focus. Unless your business is one that caters to fans, or whose demographic matches closely with the demographic of a specific show, don't waste your time.

- **Plaxo Premium (synchronization):** One of the interesting capabilities of Plaxo is its Windows (and Mac) downloadable programs, which synchronize your Microsoft Outlook contacts and calendar to your (nonpublic) Plaxo site, as well as to other online calendars, including Google's. Premium carries a low annual fee and provides a few additional bells and whistles. Our recommendation, though, is to skip this one completely and stick to the free service.

- **Plaxo Pro:** This upgrade is designed to provide better access to the Plaxo database itself, through direct messages to nonconnected members, and more search results in each search. It is priced between $20 and $250 per month, depending on the level of access desired. This might be worthwhile as a recruitment tool, or for sales executives who are searching for leads. Our recommendation: If you were going to make this type of monthly investment, we would first consider LinkedIn's paid accounts, which are about the same cost, but offer a far bigger recruit or prospect pool. (If you are unable to find whom you want within LinkedIn, then this might be a good supplementary database of names and connections.)

- **Privacy:** On most Social Media sites, it is just about impossible to figure out what is public, what is completely private, and what your connections are able to see. One of the more useful features of Plaxo solves this specific issue: You can use a drop-down menu to see your page exactly as others see it. After you load all of your information online, but before you ask for connections, this is something that you must review carefully. Fifteen minutes may save a huge amount of embarrassment.

To the extent that you have connections on Plaxo, it's worthwhile using the service—but not aggressively, unless your target audience is on the service. We recommend the basics:

- Develop your profile, with links back to your company Web site.

- Auto-fill your content from other Social Media sites—especially the company blog.

- Respond to connection requests, and possibly make some of your own.

- Search for your company name to see who is using it (and how it is being used). If it is used inappropriately, then address the issue.

Naymz

One of the benefits—and challenges—of Social Media is that each person can connect, fairly easily, to literally thousands of others. We might not know them, and we might not know their reputation. Are they really who they say they are? Can they be trusted? Who vouches for them? These are the problems that Naymz (Figure 12.3) was trying to solve; what differentiates Naymz is its concept of "*RepScore.*"

Naymz aims to capture a person's reputation by giving RepScore points for a number of different activities:

Figure 12.3. Naymz is an online Social Networking platform aimed at professionals.

- Completeness of profile

- Recent updates

- Other users vouching for you ("Community Verification")

- External authentication of identity.

In addition, your contacts can assess (e.g., rate), endorse (e.g., appear on the site), or reference you. While Plaxo has removed recommendation/endorsement functionality, this is at the center of Naymz's Community Verification.

The more points you obtain relative to other people, the higher your Rep-Score level. The system has RepScore levels from 1 to 10. Once you get to levels 9 and 10, you are rewarded with better reporting and Google ads with your name, and, presumably, more trust.

Like most of the other Social Media sites, Naymz allows you to upload your contact database from a Webmail provider (Gmail, Hotmail, Yahoo!, etc.), as well as from your desktop (Microsoft Outlook).

> **Timesaver**
>
> *Naymz also allows you to transfer your contacts and your profile information from LinkedIn, which should significantly simplify set-up.*

In the first paragraph of this section, we say "this was the problem that Naymz *was* trying to solve" because Naymz also recently added a slew of features, and changed the default homepage to emphasize its Network Feed: On login it now looks like the Plaxo Pulse, Facebook Wall, etc. While its Network Feed might be useful to those who aren't on any of the other Social Media platforms, it just dilutes its main differentiator and makes it look like a "me-too" site.

Unfortunately, the concept of company reputation is not yet developed. In the Naymz site, the "Company" is the collection of everyone who at one time had worked at (or currently works at) the organization, along with several other bits of information that you can add on your own.

Naymz has several other interesting features, including the ability to search by company, search for jobs (the jobs are sourced from *www.indeed.com*), and search on "exchanges" (status updates). By searching on exchanges, you can review who precisely had commented about your company, competitor, product, etc., in much the same way that Twitter Search allows you to do.

> **Watch Out!**
>
> *Any person who is an employee or former employee can change the company profile, including the logo, description—even the company name itself. The "changed" company name then appears on each person's individual profile—no matter what he or she originally entered.*

Xing

Based in Europe (Germany/Austria/Switzerland) and translated into many languages, Xing is an example of a more regionally focused Social Media platform. While it currently has "only" 8 million members, for those organizations focused in Europe, those 8 million might be exactly the right people.

With so many Social Media sites that exist, it is sometimes too easy to dismiss the smaller, more focused ones. The larger ones may represent a bigger pond to draw from, but they may also generate a far greater amount of noise. If your company operates in different countries (or industries), ask your local contacts what Social Media sites are locally popular—or are popular within that industry.

Xing has the standard features that one would expect: profiles, email, contacts, groups, events, jobs, and companies. It also has a very inexpensive premium level of membership that allows you to send messages to noncontacts, gets rid of advertising, and adds several other features.

Xing has a number of job posting options, including pay-per-click, text ads, and fully formatted ads, all at different price points. While the cost can be very low, Xing does not have a robust applicant-tracking system (like LinkedIn), which means that you will receive responses via email—very inefficient!

Like LinkedIn, it also provides the ability to post premium company pages; several large German companies have used this for alumni, recruiting, investor relations, etc. Again, if this is your market, an investment might make sense; if not, don't waste your time. Note that if two Xing members have individual profiles that use the same company name, then Xing automatically creates a very basic company profile page.

Xing also allows applications to be embedded. Some will be familiar to LinkedIn users, such as Slideshare or Huddle Workspaces; others not so much so. To the extent that you can use these applications to pull your already-existing content into Xing, it makes sense to do so.

One annoyance using the site is that from time to time the language defaults back to German. Jawohl!

Wikis

A Wiki is software that lets the untrained user create pages, link to other pages within the Wiki, and modify pages. The software keeps track of all changes, and who made them. The beauty of the Wiki is the distributed nature of the system: The Wiki grows organically, based on the knowledge and needs of those who add to it.

Wikipedia is by far the largest Wiki in the world, with over 85,000 contributors and 14 million articles. If you are interested in investigating how a Wiki works generally, check out *www.wikipedia.org.*

The challenge with Wikis, however, is that most are not easy to use, and they require the contributors to be trained. For this reason, Wikis are usually more effective if used for a single purpose, and with a small number of trained contributors or editors. Once there is a critical mass of information on the Wiki, then it can be opened up for others to contribute. We don't recommend starting a Wiki unless it is extremely well thought out. If it isn't, your support costs will eat up any of the benefits you were hoping for.

If you are still interested in looking at them, then a list of Wiki software can be found by searching for "Wiki software list" on Wikipedia itself.

Advanced Tip

Search on your company name to see if anyone has used it in an article. If there are inaccuracies, then you are personally empowered to make the change. If there is no entry at all, then you are empowered to add one.

Digg

Digg (Figure 12.4) is a Social Media venue where people share content from anywhere on the Web. It is more a social news site than a Social Networking site. Everything on Digg—news, photos, videos, etc.—is submitted by the Digg community. Once something is submitted, it can be viewed by others and they have the opportunity to "digg it" or not. The more "diggs" your content receives, the better your chances to have it promoted to the front page where the millions of Digg visitors can access it.

To participate, you need to become a Digg member. This is free and easy to do at the *http://www.digg.com* site. Only once you are a member can you "digg" or endorse others' submissions and submit your own content for others to (hopefully) "digg."

You can submit content like articles, blog posts, images, and videos to Digg for member review. You can also download the **Digg icons** to your Web site or blog to make it easy for your visitors to participate.

Digg enables you to send a "Shout" out to your Digg friends whenever you make a submission, making it easy for them to know when you have something new that they can "digg." They will also follow the link from Digg to your content, thus generating traffic to your site, blog, or other Social Media venue.

Digg icons

These are small icons that appear on your site (or blog) that let users easily bookmark that page's content onto Digg.

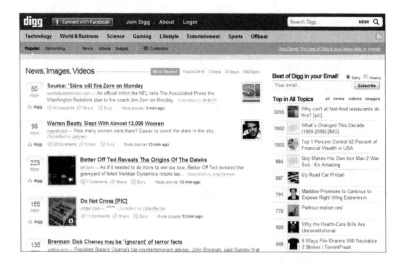

Figure 12.4.   Digg is a popular social news Web site where the content is provided—and voted on—by the users.

The search engines index Digg content, providing an additional benefit.

If you get to the home page of Digg, you will see massive exposure and significant traffic. At any time, there are anywhere from 10 to 20 stories on the home page, and they stay there for a few hours until other content replaces them.

The type of content that gets to the home page is similar to what gets to the front page of a newspaper:

- Breaking news

- How-to articles

- Heart-warming stories

- Upcoming events.

Digg evangelists will generally have a strategy to:

- Maximize the number of Digg friends

- Incorporate the Digg icons on their Web site or blog

- Promote their Digg submissions through their Social Media venues, newsletters, ezines, signature files, etc.

- Maximize the SEO opportunity by incorporating appropriate keyword phrases and links.

Del.icio.us

Del.icio.us is a social bookmarking service that is owned by Yahoo! and allows you to store your favorite sites. You can also **tag** these sites for quick reference and share them with others. Del.icio.us has a number of features like networks, tags, tag bundles, and subscriptions.

Tag

To identify a picture or content with a descriptive word or a person's name.

To participate, you set up your free account, which takes only a few minutes at *http://delicious.com*. Once you have registered, you can start bookmarking your favorite sites and sharing them with your friends.

You can build your bookmarks and you can import any bookmarks or favorites you have stored in your Web browser. When you bookmark a Web page on Del.icio.us, you tag it with keywords that describe the content.

When tagging, you should use words that make sense to you but also make sense to others you will be sharing the bookmarks with. You can use multiple tags for any site you save. You can always edit, add, or delete tags at a later time.

Del.icio.us has a number of tools that allow you to share your bookmarks with friends and other Del.icio.us users. You can provide a link to all of your bookmarks with *http://www.delicious.com/username* or through an icon on your Web site or blog. You can encourage others to subscribe to your RSS feed. You can create a Del.icio.us network, which is a page of several Del.icio.us users' bookmarks.

You can find others' great bookmarks in a number of ways. You can check out the Fresh and Popular bookmarks on the Del.icio.us home page. You can click on the Explore Tags button and put in any term in the "type a tag" area to find others' bookmarks that they have tagged with that keyword. You can use tag subscription, which alerts you every time someone bookmarks a site and uses that tag.

You can bundle your tags, making it easier for you and others to find relevant bookmarked sites. For example, you can bundle "SEO articles" and "SEO tools" under "SEO Resources."

You should add the Del.icio.us "Save this Page" icon on your blog and Web site to encourage your blog and Web site visitors to add it to their bookmarks.

Sharing Tools

You want to make it easy for others to share or otherwise promote your content. If it's not easy to do, it won't get done. Fortunately, there are several free tools that you can use to add a button to your Web site or blog that enables visitors to share your content anywhere and everywhere they want. One popular tool for this is AddThis (*http://www.addthis.com*) (Figure 12.5). It literally takes seconds at the AddThis Web site to design the icon or button and get the code to add to your Web site or blog. This tool is free. It automatically optimizes itself for each visitor's preferences and language.

A similar tool is called ShareThis (*http://www.sharethis.com*). ShareThis (Figure 12.6) is also a widget that lets visitors share your content with all of their profiles, blogs, friends, and contacts. It is also compatible with most of the popular social networks and email options, including Facebook, Twitter, Digg, MySpace, and many others.

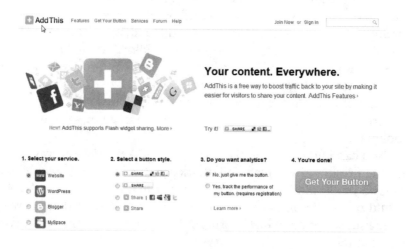

Figure 12.5. AddThis is a popular free tool to add social bookmarking to your site, blog, or Social Media applications.

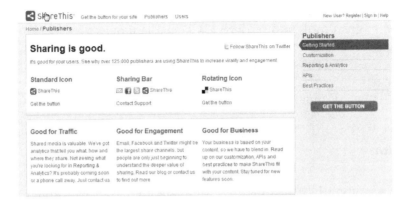

Figure 12.6. ShareThis is another popular free tool to add social bookmarking to your site, blog, or Social Media applications.

First Steps

1. Learn about which Second-Tier Social Media sites your customers, suppliers, job candidates, and other stakeholders are using via market research, informal conversations, and company or product name searches on a selection of these sites. Determine which of these are worthy of your time—and how you might measure your success with them.

2. Ensure that you are using either AddThis or ShareThis (or a similar tool) on your blog and Web site.

Additional Resources

Here are some additional resources that you may find useful.

Software/Tools

- The sites listed in the introduction to this chapter are all linked from the book's companion Web site.

- Susan and Randall are always updating their social bookmarks with great tools and resources. Check them out at Diigo:

  - Susan's are available at *www.diigo.com/user/susansweeney.*

  - Randall's are available *www.diigo.com/user/RandallCraig.*

Education

- Susan has ongoing live webinars and recorded online courses on this topic available through the webinars and online store at her site, *http://www.susansweeney.com,* and provides access to others' courses on the subject through her online learning portal, eLearningU, at *http://www.elearningu.com.*

- Randall delivers workshops and webinars on this and related Social Media topics, all available at *www.RandallCraig.com.*

13

Other Sites

Overview

Among the many Social Media sites, there are a number that you might not immediately consider to be Social Media at all. Yet during the past few years, and for obvious marketing reasons, each has worked hard to embed this type of functionality. This trend is unlikely to stop: Social Media effectively has become the new normal in the marketing world, and certainly so on the Web.

eBay

The world's largest and most ubiquitous auction marketplace, eBay (*www.eBay. com*) was one of the first companies to use Social Media.

At the core of eBay's business was the issue of trust. Think about it: In the real world, you walk into a store, choose what you want to purchase, and then walk to the cashier to exchange your money for the item you've selected.

When catalogs were first distributed several generations ago, the reputation of the catalog seller was the guarantee that you would receive your merchandise. When retailers began selling online, there was little change, as the trust

Figure 13.1. eBay enables you to customize your personal profile.

relationship was still one seller to many buyers. And because the transactions used credit cards, if need be, there was always third-party recourse in case of dispute.

The genius of eBay is that it was the first retailer to solve the many-to-many trust problem, by providing a mechanism for buyers and sellers to assess the counterparty early in the transaction process. Both buyers and sellers worked hard for good ratings: Bad ratings meant fewer bids and higher transaction risk.

Overall, consider the Social Media elements within eBay:

- A personal profile gets created for each user, which is customizable (see Figure 13.1) with additional content.

- Users can list items to sell (the ultimate in user-generated content!).

- Users can bid on listed items.

- Comments get traded during the transaction.

- Users rate and comment on each others' experience at the transaction conclusion.

- There are groups and "neighborhoods."

- Chat rooms are available.

One interesting use for eBay is to create a fan base for your older "classic" products. This can be done by setting up a group for this purpose and then reaching out to past buyers and sellers to alert them to it. Note that to start a group you need a certain amount of transaction feedback.

If any members of your company's senior management team use eBay, and their username is very close to their real name, there is a risk that this information might appear elsewhere . . . like in the press. Best check to see if there is anything embarrassing, and deal with it privately.

Watch Out!

A user's profile page and any transaction feedback given or received is public.

Answers Sites

There are many sites that allow users to post questions and receive answers from other members of that community. The best-known ones are Yahoo! Answers (answers.yahoo.com), Answers.com, Askville (see Figure 13.2) by Amazon (www.Askville.com), Answerbag.com, Askpedia.com, and several others.

The sites are all relatively similar: The user asks a question, which is then posted in a place where others can share their experience. To provide incentive, some sites give points for best answer or most answers, allowing a reputation to develop over time. In addition, these sites allow users to search the database of answered questions.

Very similar to the strategy suggested for LinkedIn, we see very little benefit in spending a large amount of time on these sites for the purpose of developing reputation. Yet there is an opportunity to showcase your company by virtue of the answers you provide to certain select questions. When people search on this topic, your answer will appear. Note that blatant commercial messaging is always frowned upon and would likely result in the exact opposite impact that you want.

Another great use for answers sites is research and development. Reviewing the questions and answers in your product or service area will likely expose needs that currently are not being met. Or a review might expose alternate product uses, new marketing messaging, or an early warning of a competitive trend.

On each of the answers sites, there are a number of users who have taken to answering questions as a hobby. These are incredibly powerful influencers, not unlike the bloggers whose blogs also generate a following. If you are able

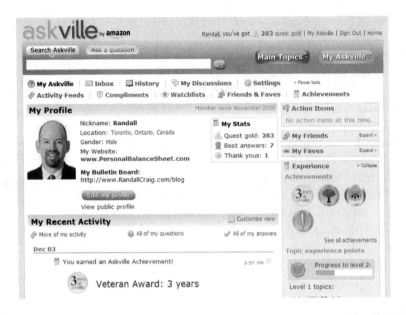

Figure 13.2.   Askville is one site where you can ask questions or provide answers. (Yahoo! is another.)

to identify who the influential answerers are, then you may be able to provide them additional support: a direct link to your second-level support, product samples, etc.

Ratings Sites

Some Web sites (e.g., Amazon, Barnes & Noble, Travelocity) are big enough marketplaces to gather product feedback and ratings directly from their customers. In fact, they are big enough that they are even able to ask their users to rate the raters!

In other cases, entire sites are devoted to collecting product and service feedback. Sites such as epinions.com, alatest.com, and viewpoints.com collect user feedback and (sometimes) marry it with a shopping comparison service.

The reason these sites are so successful is clear: Before spending money, people do their research. They ask their friends, family, and colleagues for recommendations. Because these contacts are trusted, so are their recommendations. There's little need for corroboration.

With ratings sites, the user doesn't know the raters, so the element of trust seems to be removed. Yet, users can still look at the points that each reviewer makes and decide for themselves whether or not they are valid. When there are a large number of reviews, the user can further rely on the law of large numbers: If most of the reviewers say a product is good, then it probably is. (They can also rely on the ratings of the reviews.)

You may be tempted to write glowing reviews on your product, or to ask your marketing agency to do so for you. Don't. Imagine the public embarrassment if this became known. All it takes is one disgruntled employee, or one sharp journalist, and the story is out. A far more pragmatic approach is to engage the reviewer directly, or become part of the exchange by writing your response as a follow-up review. Monitoring the ratings sites is critical, as these pages fare very well in Google search results.

Like the answers sites, ratings sites are also a source of market research and market intelligence. If the reviewers all point out a specific deficiency, or if they all laud a feature that only your competitor has, wouldn't your product development people want to know about it? Or better yet, wouldn't they want to be part of the dialogue directly?

Depending on your industry, ratings sites may be less or more important. Generally, the higher the ticket price, or the more a person cares about a purchase, the more investigation will be done—and the more people would be willing to actually write a review. Industries such as travel, bookselling, automotive, and electronics fall into this category. Products that are commodities rarely have ratings.

Yahoo!

Yahoo! began its venerable existence as a directory of Web sites, back in the mid-1990s. It worked hard to become the home page of choice for users: adding specialized content, email, news, games, and, at this point, just about everything.

Part of that everything is advertising; part is Social Media functionality, including Profiles, Flickr, HotJobs (now owned by Monster.com), instant messaging, discussion groups, ecards, shopping, and more. As a conglomerate, Yahoo! can expect the list of functionality to change over time: new functionality added and other parts sold or shut down.

One of the best strategic decisions that Yahoo! has made has been to make deals with residential Internet service providers to take over the email, profile, and portal or home page services. This has locked in a huge number of users who see the Yahoo! home page, use Yahoo! Search, and all of the other Yahoo! services.

For small businesses, Yahoo! is hoping to sell its search engine marketing services, HotJobs job-posting service, Web hosting, and e-commerce services. On the advertising front, Microsoft and Yahoo! have inked a search advertising partnership deal, where a purchase on one system will result in placement on both.

There are several non-advertising-related opportunities, however, that you should be aware of:

- **Yahoo! Directory:** The directory actually still exists. If you are a noncommercial Web site, there is no charge to have your site listed. Commercial sites must pay a recurring annual fee (about $300) to appear. Unless you think your target user base uses the Yahoo! Directory, don't waste your time or money: Most people now look for Web sites using search engines, and Google in particular.

- **Yahoo! Search Engine Submission:** At no cost, you are able to submit your Web site, mobile site, and even your media content directly to Yahoo!'s search engine or directly to Microsoft's Bing search engine, which powers Yahoo! search. (While it is true that the Yahoo! Search may come across your Web site or blog eventually, manually submitting it guarantees that it will be in the search index.)

- **Product and Travel Submissions:** If you want your products to appear in Yahoo! Shopping or Yahoo! Travel Deals, you are able to use a "pay-per-click" model. This is worth testing if your company sells to consumers.

Advanced Tip

Yahoo! provides a way to improve how your search results are shown, just by adding a few lines of HTML code to each of your Web pages. If you have a strong Webmaster, tell him or her to look for SearchMonkey in the Yahoo! Developer Network. Note: As part of the Microsoft-Yahoo! search marketing partnership, Yahoo! is adopting Microsoft's Bing search engine in place of its own; when this occurs, SearchMonkey functionality may no longer be recognized.

- **Yahoo! Local:** At no cost, you can create a listing for your real-world location, complete with contact information, address, and a link to your Web site. This is easy to do, but instructions are hidden in an obscure place; go to *local.yahoo.com* and scroll to the bottom of the page. Look for the headline "*Local Resources*" and click "*Add a Business.*"

- **Yahoo! Upcoming** (*upcoming.yahoo.com*): If your business is event-based, listing your events on this service can promote them, as well as generate some discussion or comments.

- **Yahoo! Groups:** If you are looking for a way to host a private online group, complete with calendar, mailing list, discussion forum, file storage, etc., then Yahoo! Groups might be worth looking into. The price is right (free), and Yahoo! Groups can be set up with very little technical knowledge. The advantage of using Yahoo! over a LinkedIn group is the additional functionality, notably file storage. The main disadvantage is that it is not as tightly connected to a core Social Media engine: Most people don't have robust profiles on Yahoo!, but they do have them on LinkedIn. If you're interested in Yahoo! Groups, also look at Google Groups, which provides similar functionality.

MSN/Windows Live

MSN (*www.msn.com*) is another of the Internet's major portals, created and managed by Microsoft. Like Yahoo!, it has literally dozens of subsites, news, careers, games, and other services. It also has other Microsoft properties, including built-in MSN Messenger, Hotmail, and the Bing search engine. The branding has changed numerous times, and this portal is now part of the "Windows Live" experience.

Windows Live itself includes most of Microsoft's Social Media functionality, including profiles, photos, groups, calendars, "Spaces" (blog), events, groups, and "SkyDrive" (file storage). Similar to Facebook, MySpace, and many of the other Social Media sites, Windows Live shows a stream of activity from your network.

Like the other Social Media sites, if your target audiences spend time on MSN/Windows Live, then it is worthwhile considering. And like Yahoo!, there are numerous advertising options also available—not just Social Media.

What is interesting with Windows Live is where Microsoft is hoping to take it in the future. The Windows Live ID is an identity that can be used on its Xbox Live video game system. An online version of Microsoft Office uses the same identity management. One would think that a connection within the Windows Live ecosystem might provide access to business users, sometime in the future. Our recommendation, however, is to proceed with extreme caution: There has been a history of mid-course changes with Microsoft's strategy. Speculative "investment" here is a long shot with risk.

Ning and SocialGo

So far, many of the strategies reviewed require participation on an external site: Facebook, LinkedIn, YouTube, etc. The expression *"Fish where the fish are"* defines these strategies: Instead of trying to reel users in to your Web site, you go to their Social Media neighborhoods, "setting up shop" with fan pages, groups, and the like.

Ning, SocialGo, and several like it are completely different. They are platforms for you to construct your very own Social Media site. Think of it: your own branded Social Media site, with all the functionality found in Facebook, MySpace, or LinkedIn. The only thing they don't provide is a user base.

With both sites (Ning and SocialGo), you can join other people's public networks, or you can create one of your own. Both systems have a free and a premium-paid version. On Ning, for example, depending on how much you pay each month, you can use your own domain name, remove advertising, and use more bandwidth and storage. SocialGo does the same, but also adds features to allow for member billing.

When setting up the site, you will have an option to make it private—hidden from all but invitees—or public—available to everybody. Both have their uses. Private sites can be for top-tier clients, your suppliers, or your former employees. Public sites might be for prospective and existing customers.

The Ning network shown in Figure 13.3 is for chapter presidents of the National Speakers Association. It doesn't get more specific than that!

Figure 13.3. Ning is a platform for creating your own Social Network.

The advantage of having your own network is that you can make it tightly focused on an important business priority. Of course, the narrower the site focus, the fewer users you will attract, and the tougher it will be to find them. Yet, those whom you do attract will have a higher degree of loyalty than a typical user from a public network such as LinkedIn or Facebook.

These networks do have a downside: They are walled gardens. They may provide beautiful functionality on the inside, but they don't play well with others. What happens, for example, if you want to extract all of the conversations, profiles, groups, and other resources? It's just about impossible. More tough questions: Who precisely owns the content? Does the Social Media platform company (Ning or SocialGo) have the right to use "your" names for their own marketing purposes? And what happens to "your" site if they go bankrupt? Read the fine print!

Assuming that you decided to build a network on one of these platforms, here is the process:

> **Watch Out!**
>
> *The terms and conditions governing these sites change from time to time—often not in your favor. Yes, read the fine print, but keep doing it every six months or so, just in case.*

1. Search to see if someone else has taken your idea. If you are both fighting for the same people, it will be a drawn-out, draining, and discouraging war of attrition. Find a way to differentiate—and distinguish—your proposed initiative from others.

2. Register, and choose the functionality that you wish to enable. We recommend that you go with one of the paid options, if only to remove the advertising and be able to use your own domain name.

3. Pre-seed the site with content from your company and from "friends" of your company.

4. Send general invitations for other users to join. This is more effective if they are given a taste of the content that will await them if they register. (This might mean giving away a whitepaper or ebook, or it may mean highlighting the names of well-known contributors.)

5. Add the widget (an interactive advertisement) from the site onto your other Web properties to gather more users.

6. Finally, you'll want to contribute to the conversation yourself, monitor postings, and continue to market the site, both online and offline.

Google

Google is the elephant in the room. While most people may use Google's search engine, the number of innovative Web applications they have spawned is tremendous. What is interesting is how quickly so many of these have developed a Social Media or collaborative hook. Consider some of what they do:

- **YouTube:** This is a video-sharing service, now with the ability for users to comment, rate, follow, and subscribe.

- **Picasa:** This service offers photo sharing; it is very similar to Yahoo!'s Flickr.

- **Feedburner:** This adds more functionality, and tracking, to your blogs.

- **Places:** Connect your physical location to Google location-based search results; you can also add coupons, which appear alongside your search results in Google Maps. (Note that people can also rate and comment about your business.)

- **Orkut:** Popular South American (and Indian) Social Network, similar to Facebook. Gmail contacts can be Orkut "friends."

- **Profiles:** This can incorporate photos from popular photo-sharing sites; you have control over who can see what information you post.

Watch Out!

Search for your business within Google Maps, and when you find it, you'll want to "Claim Your Business." If you don't do this, someone else can.

- **Buzz:** This is very similar to Twitter or Facebook's wall, except that it is completely integrated into Gmail.

- **Lattitude:** This is a system that relies on the GPS within your phone that plots your physical location—and your friends—on a map.

- **Google Docs:** This is a Web-based spreadsheet, word processor, and presentation program that is designed to compete with Microsoft Office. What makes these unique is that groups of people can collaborate on the documents, making changes to the same document simultaneously.

- **Calendar:** This is a Web-based calendar that others can share (if you wish).

- **Groups:** Very similar functionality to Yahoo! groups: You can join a public group or create your own public or private group. This is better than Yahoo! for discussions, but less functional for file organization, and it has no built-in calendaring. (Google Calendar can be used, but strangely, it currently isn't integrated.)

- **Google Wave:** This is a Social Media-based discussion group, document, and messaging system, designed to help individuals collaborate in real time. It is relatively new, but promising.

- **Google Android and Chrome OS:** Android is Google's mobile phone-based operating system, and Chrome OS is Google's operating system for laptops and desktops. While these by themselves are not Social Media platforms, they are examples of Google's reach—right down to the operating system itself. Over the next few years, expect some of Google's innovation to first appear (or be tested) on Android or Chrome OS—and then elsewhere.

Probably one of the most interesting Google innovations is Google FriendConnect. Like the Facebook version of this, it involves adding some HTML code to your Web site, which allows users to use their Google profile to become a "member" of your site. Unlike Ning or SocialGo, which are merely links to your Web site, Google FriendConnect is embedded completely within it.

Depending on what Google FriendConnect modules you choose to implement, users can participate in discussions, rate page content, post recommendations, subscribe to newsletters, and more. On the back end, there are analytics to allow you to understand more about your users and their preferences. Google FriendConnect is an interesting way to bring Social Media features to even the most staid of Web sites, without an expensive technology overhaul.

First Steps

1. As you spend time on your favorite Web sites, whether it be a news site, a shopping site, or a customer's or supplier's site, consider how they have used Social Media techniques—and how you might use their experience for your benefit.

2. Consider the question: Does it make more sense to latch onto a "public" Social Media site (such as LinkedIn, Facebook, etc.), create your own (Ning or SocialGo), or embed Social Media functionality within your regular site (e.g., Facebook Open Graph or Google FriendConnect)?

Additional Resources

Here are some additional resources that you may find useful.

Software/Tools

- The sites listed in the introduction to this chapter are all linked from the book's companion Web site.

- Susan and Randall are always updating their social bookmarks with great tools and resources. Check them out at Diigo:

  - Susan's are available at *www.diigo.com/user/susansweeney*.

  - Randall's are available at *www.diigo.com/user/RandallCraig*.

- Mashable's Google Social Media page is located at www.mashable.com/social-media/google.

Books

- *Ultimate Guide to Google AdWords,* 2nd Edition, January 2010
  This book, now in its second edition, gives comprehensive guidance and strategy for Google AdWords advertising. While it's not Social Media-focused, for those who are interested, it's a great place to start.

Education

- Susan has ongoing live webinars and recorded online courses on this topic available through the webinars and online store at her site, *http://www.susansweeney.com*, and provides access to others' courses on the subject through her online learning portal, eLearningU, at *http://www. elearningu.com.*

- Randall delivers workshops and webinars on this and related Social Media topics, all available at *www.RandallCraig.com.*

14

Mobile Access

Overview

Who is using their mobile device for Social Media these days? Well, users are all over the map in terms of adoption. We have some users with mobile devices that don't have the capability to surf the Web, we have users with the technology but not the interest or inclination, we have users who sporadically and selectively use their mobile device to access the internet, and then we have others still who do everything on their mobile device and rarely go to their computers anymore. Many younger people with no computer on their desk but an iPhone on their hip feel very comfortable with this technology.

No longer do we have to sit in front of our computers to participate in our Social Media conversations. Facebook, Twitter, and many social venues have apps that are optimized to work with mobile devices; so, have phone will travel.

Interesting Stats

Users of iPhone and BlackBerry have completely different experiences when using their mobile devices. The iPhone users surf and use applications more. Interesting statistics: According to Morgan Stanley's Mobile Internet Report, the iPhone

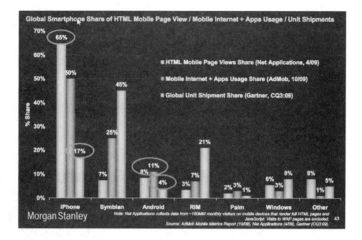

Figure 14.1. Morgan Stanley's Mobile Internet Report shows the iPhone with 65 percent of all HTML mobile page views—yet the iPhone has only 17 percent of the global unit shipment share.

has a relatively small global unit shipment share of 17 percent but a staggering 65 percent of all HTML mobile page views share (Figure 14.1).

Another interesting statistic from Morgan Stanley's report: 58 percent of iPhone users do social networking through their mobile device as compared to 14 percent of the average mobile users and 43 percent of Smartphone users (Figure 14.2).

According to a recent IDC survey report, more than 50 percent of respondents in China, India, South Korea, and Thailand access social networks via mobile phones. In China and Thailand, 62 percent and 65 percent of the survey respondents use mobile phones to get news alerts and notifications, receive and reply to messages, upload photos, or update personal status and profiles on popular Social Networking sites.

Applications

With the internet, we went from Web sites where people visited us to get information, to permission-based marketing where we pushed the information to our target market, to social marketing where we have two-way communication. We

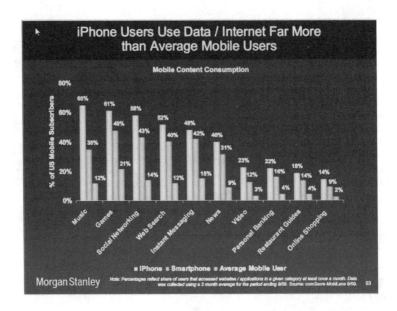

Figure 14.2. According to Morgan Stanley's Internet Report, 58 percent of iPhone users do Social Networking through their mobile device.

have seen the same evolution with the mobile phone. First it was for telephone conversations, then it moved to permission-based communication where we gave

Armani

A few years ago, I was shopping at Armani in South Beach. On checking out, the clerk asked if I wanted to save on my purchase. . . . Well, yeah. All I had to do was text Armani (giving permission for future texts to me I am sure, but who reads that stuff when you're at the checkout with a lineup) and I received an immediate response via text on my cell with the discount code that I had to provide to the cashier to receive my discount on that day's purchase. Every 10 days or so I was provided additional information on hot deals.

permission to businesses to send updates and promotions to our mobile devices, and now with the Social Media boom we are seeing two-way communication explode.

Today the number of applications available on our mobile devices that enable us to communicate, market, and sell has gone through the roof. If you can think it, there is probably an app that can do it. These go from the simple straightforward uses of technology to the "Amazing—how'd they do that!!" applications.

We have all seen the simple things like picture and video upload applications to enable us to send those media directly to our blog, Flickr, Facebook, and Twitter.

- Google Latitude is a tool that allows you to see where your friends are on a map and provides the capability to contact them with **SMS**, IM, or a phone call. You can control your location and who gets to see it.

SMS (short message service)

Otherwise known as "texting" from a mobile device.

- With Bump (Figure 14.3), you can "bump" two phones (currently works on the iPhone and Android) together and swap all or some of your contacts complete with photos. Contact information is saved directly into the address books, and photos are saved directly to the camera roll of both participants in the swap. It's a 1-2-3 process: (1) Open Bump on both phones. (2) While holding the phones, gently bump your hands together. And (3) Confirm the exchange.

- Red Laser is an iPhone barcode scanner. Once you download this app, you can scan an item in a store with your iPhone camera and instantly have access to comparative online prices and information. Scan a book barcode and check for online reviews.

- Twitter360 is an iPhone app that lets you visually see the flow of tweets from locations nearby.

Augmented Reality is taking on a life of its own. John Cox, in a recent article in Network World, defines Augmented Reality (AR) this way, "Augmented Reality is a coalescing of technologies that promises to create a new interactive

Figure 14.3. Bump enables Smartphones to swap all or some of their contacts, complete with photos, by "bumping" the phones together.

relationship between mobile users and their surroundings." He goes on to further describe the technology: "You're able to augment the reality you see with data drawn from a variety of different online sources, such as Wikipedia, YouTube, Flickr, or commercial content providers."

Apps are already developed to overlay restaurant information, ATM locations, and to access information from the social-ranking site Yelp; and the Wikitude World Browser presents users with data about their surroundings, nearby landmarks, and other points of interest by overlaying information on the real-time camera view of an iPhone.

There are over 140,000 iPhone applications alone. Take some time to sift through and become familiar with the types of applications your customers, your suppliers, and your competitors are using.

Mobile Capabilities Now and in the Near Future

Some things have gone from the Web to the mobile device, others have gone from the mobile device to the Web, and some things are for the mobile device only.

The capabilities of the mobile device are escalating rapidly. With each new feature, there seems to be additional Social Media and Social Networking capabilities and opportunities. Features today and tomorrow include:

- Camera

- Video

- GPS

- Compass

- Distant video surveillance

- Mobile TV

- Global roaming

- Video on demand

- Mobile video conferences

- Remote control of household appliances

- Mobile commerce

- Multi-channel hi-fi television broadcasts.

First Steps

1. Familiarize yourself with the mobile space. What's happening and what are the opportunities in your industry? What are the leaders in your industry doing? What is your target market using?

2. Determine what your competition is doing and what their plans are in the mobile space.

3. For most businesses, you want to develop your strategy to be leading edge—not bleeding edge where you must educate consumers before you can engage them.

Additional Resources

Here are some additional resources that you may find useful.

Software/Tools

- For iPhones and iPhone apps, the best place to look is iTunes. Even if you don't have an iPhone yourself, downloading the free iTunes software and going into the iTunes store to look will give you some great ideas. At the time of publication, there were significantly more iPhone apps than Android, Palm Pre, or Microsoft apps, which is why we are recommending that you look there first.

- Susan and Randall are always updating their social bookmarks with great tools and resources. Check them out at Diigo:

  - Susan's are available at *www.diigo.com/user/susansweeney*.

    – Randall's are available at *www.diigo.com/user/RandallCraig.*

- Mashable's mobile Social Media page is located at *www.mashable.com/ mobile.*

Books

- *Mobile Marketing: Finding Your Customers No Matter Where They Are,* by Cindy Krum, March 2010
  This book of over 300 pages provides detailed information on mobile marketing strategy and how to integrate it with other marketing initiatives.

Education

- Susan has ongoing live webinars and recorded online courses on this topic available through the webinars and online store at her site, *http:// www.susansweeney.com*, and provides access to others' courses on the subject through her online learning portal, eLearningU, at *http://www. elearningu.com.*

- Randall delivers workshops and webinars on this and related Social Media topics, all available at *www.RandallCraig.com.*

15

Tactical Ideas

This chapter is designed to expose you to the extremely wide variety of existing Social Media opportunities. This list certainly isn't exhaustive, and every idea can be implemented in untold variations.

Many of the ideas fit into several categories. For example, participating in industry forums and discussion groups might be great customer service, but also great for marketing and new product development.

The ideas presented are quite broad; some are designed to be added to existing Web initiatives, others are stand-alone campaigns, mobile strategies, etc. Some may appear quite exciting, but before you rush to implement one, first consider how it fits within your overall plan: The Social Media priority planner, described in detail in the next chapter, will help you do this.

Sales

- Embed cross-selling functionality into your Web site, based on real customer data: "Customers who bought [this] bought [that]."

- Embed recommendations functionality into your Web site, based on real customer data: "Customers who looked at [this] also looked at [that]."

- Embed wish lists into your Web site, with the ability to share the wish list with friends.

- Allow your customers to put together product lists and their own recommendations; think of it as personalized shareable best-seller lists.

- Create an interview show (audio or video) featuring the product and how it can be used.

- Tweet time-limited discount codes to your followers. Advertise this offline.

- Tweet limited availability of your products or services. "52 widgets left" . . . "available tee times" . . . etc.

- Create a quiz for sales representatives on product benefits; allow them to share with their clients and prospects.

Affiliate

A term used to describe others who sell your products on their Web sites, for a small commission.

- Pay an **affiliate** commission to those who recommend your product in their blog and provide a link to your shopping cart page. (Note that this will require disclosure on their blog.)

- Create an internal sales mentorship blog that allows experienced sales and marketing professionals to share their expertise with newer hires.

- Develop an iPhone, Android, Blackberry or Palm "app" that provides details on your products or services—and connects your experience using them with other, similar users. Leverage this further by embedding links to initiate a sale.

- Solicit, and then embed, product testimonials within the shopping cart upsell and checkout pages.

- Incorporate "Tell a Friend" elements related to your products, services, specials, packages, coupons, discounts, contests, and new products.

- Provide a password for limited-time specials on your Facebook page.

- Tweet great deals that are available for the next 20 customers that walk into your store and give the secret code.

Customer Service

- Solicit customers to create and share videos about the installation process.

- Start up a Ning or SocialGo network for different categories of customers.

- LinkedIn group: Set up a client page with product news, as well as support.

- Participate in industry forums and discussion groups.

- Participate in third-party forums or groups within MySpace, Facebook, and LinkedIn.

- Ask your employees to spend some time on answers sites as unofficial company representatives, responding to questions on your products and how to use them.

- Participate officially on answers sites.

Marketing: General

- Embed Social Media logos throughout your site, linking to your Social Media profiles on each platform.

- Run a contest: Facebook or Flickr tagging of the product photographed in unique locations, or used in a unique manner.

- List your Twitter accounts in directories such as wefollow.com, twellow.com, and justtweetit.com.

- Customize a game created on Facebook around the product usage.

- Customize a game created on an iPhone around the product usage, or involving photographing the product as it's being used.

- Create a podcast series featuring company personalities, products, customers, or suppliers.

- Make a paid product placement in a third-party game or virtual world.

- Include Twitter and Facebook addresses in ads, brochures, etc.

- Blog about new products.

- Tweet about new products.

- Twitter: Ask customers to describe how they use your products.

- Video: Hold a contest to create a TV (or YouTube) commercial for your product.

- Create a Facebook fan page for your products.

- Allow your customers (and others) to rank your products on your site.

- Allow your customers (and others) to write reviews of your products on your site.

- Incorporate viral marketing or "Tell a Friend" throughout your blog and Web site.

- Include Social Media links within email signatures.

- Comment on others' blog postings.

- Start a campaign to increase product sales rankings (e.g., get everyone to purchase from a particular site on one day).

- Set up online voting for corporate social responsibility funding. The Aviva Insurance company's "Aviva Community Fund" (Figure 15.1) is a great example of this. Check it out at *http://www.avivacommunityfund.org*.

- Ask your employees (and other stakeholders) to set their status to a common message on a particular day.

- Use your blog to solicit product testimonials.

- Hold a contest for the best adaptation or modification of your product.

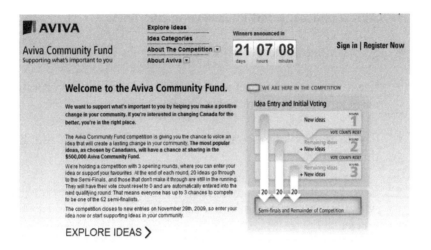

Figure 15.1. Aviva provides online voting for corporate social responsibility funding.

- Provide the ability for your customers (and others) to share their recipes, maps, or other ideas with other users.

- If your marketing initiative is national in scope, make a special deal with Facebook, MySpace, and other Social Media for special ad placement, coverage, etc.

- Pay to change the background of certain pages to include your branding.

- Give your products to prominent bloggers for their review. (Note: Recent legislation requires that they disclose the nature of any "gift" that they were given.)

- Host prominent bloggers, Tweeple, and other Social Media personalities with a behind-the-scenes tour of your production or R&D facility.

- Develop a quiz or game on end-customers' product knowledge, rewarding them for correct answers and for sharing the quiz with others.

- Create a survey on product usage by demographic.

- Start an audio podcast series interviewing people in your industry.

- Start a podcast series interviewing customers.

- Start a video podcast or "TV show."

- Use a video-syndication service so that your video is cross-posted automatically on dozens of video-sharing sites.

- Create an ebook that compiles comments from a blog, and then distribute this to a list.

- Retrofit your Web site with an "AddThis" or "ShareThis" widget. This will allow the page link to be shared via just about any Social Media service.

- Actively support "unofficial" groups devoted to your products.

- Tweet about product launches in real time.

- Develop standard hashtags for any official Tweets from your company.

- Embed widgets on your Web site(s): Twitter feed, Blog headlines, etc.

- Provide answer-site super-users with product samples, professional development, early new-product notices, etc.

- Use Twitter to take questions from the audience during a webinar.

- Use Twitter to take questions during a live presentation.

- Monitor Twitter postings during a live presentation to address audience discontent.

- Include a "Send this page to a friend" link on every page of your Web site.

PR and Crisis Management

- Develop a crisis management plan, just in case.

- Check Twitter trending topics for crisis PR early warning.

- Set up Google Alerts with the company's name, to monitor where and how your company name is being used.

- Set up Google Alerts with the names of your senior management, to alert the company to possible problems.

- Use TweetDeck, Seesmic, or HootSuite to set up and monitor Twitter searches for your company name.

- Use TweetDeck, Seesmic, or HootSuite to set up and monitor Twitter searches for the names of senior managers.

- Use targeted PPC advertisements to draw concerned people to your side of the story.

- Appoint someone who is familiar with Social Media to act as a spokesperson.

- Create unpublished fan pages within Facebook on a number of possible crisis scenarios, ready for emergency deployment.

- Crisis response: Mobilize your workforce, customers, and suppliers to rise to your defense online.

- Create a special Twitter account specifically for crises.

- Check Twitter trending topics for proactive PR opportunities.

- Officially "leak" new product plans to rumor Web sites.

- Strategically leak details about upcoming products in your blog, on Twitter, on Facebook, etc.

- Add select bloggers to your media-release distribution list.

Recruitment

- Create "Day in the life" YouTube videos for the most commonly recruited-for positions.

- Post event photos on Flickr, Facebook, MySpace.

- Create a virtual recruitment center.

- Post a new-employee blog with questions and answers.

- Post video examples of interviews.

- Participate in job search Web site blogs and discussion groups (e.g., Monster).

- Participate in career Web site blogs and discussion groups (e.g., Vault).

- Partnerships with recruitment Web sites; host the blog or moderate a forum.

- Have a "Recommend a friend" link on your Web site or blog to find new candidates.

- Post job listings on LinkedIn.

- LinkedIn: Put a link to your job posting in the groups that you belong to.

- LinkedIn: Candidate due diligence and reference-checking.

- Create a custom company page on LinkedIn.

- Advertise your company on LinkedIn.

- Run LinkedIn "talent-direct" email campaigns.

- Facebook: Run targeted pay-per-click advertisements.

- Internally: Use a Wiki as an onboarding tool.

- Send Tweets about new openings.

- Post new openings on Facebook and any other Social Media sites.

- Create a quiz: "Will you make a good employee?" Collect answers and post them online, with the demographics.

- Create a Wiki that allows all new hires to answer the question: "What can I do before I start my job to improve my success after I start?"

- Create a Wiki or blog to improve the on-boarding process; have employees write tips for the newest hires.

- Review the Social Media profiles of new recruits prior to hiring them as part of the reference checking/due diligence process.

- Write a Social Media policy guide and distribute it to all employees.

Research and Development

- Hold focus groups and interviews with prominent bloggers, Tweeple, answer-site super-users, and other Social Media personalities to get their perspective on product changes and new-product development.

- Create Tweets and blog entries calling for user feedback on current products.

- Create Tweets and blog entries asking for ideas for new products.

- Create Tweets and blog entries asking for beta testers of new products.

- Do beta testing using LinkedIn's highly targeted market research capability.

- Create user surveys (based on Twitter followers, Facebook friends, or MySpace fans) to collect data on market requirements.

- Do market research through LinkedIn's facility to highly target specific professional demographics.

- Get recommendations for existing and new products through **crowdsourcing**.

- Check Twitter trending topics for new business opportunities.

- Check answers sites for trending topics and new business opportunities.

> **Crowdsourcing**
> *To throw a question to a large group of people, and then use their feedback (and their conversations) to guide your actions.*

Training

- Create Wiki how-to's.

- Create YouTube demonstration videos.

- Ask your customers to upload their how-to videos.

- Ask your customers to upload their installation videos.

- Upload product shots to Flickr and other photo-sharing sites.

- Ask your customers to upload their photos to Flickr and other photo-sharing sites.

- Upload instruction manual chapters as blog postings, and ask your customers, installers, sales team, and engineers to add comments to the postings.

- Create a quick-tips blog or Wiki for each product; ask your service personnel to put it together.

- Create internal "just-in-time" training videos and podcasts on common company processes and systems.

- Record the Webcasts from your outside trainers and post them on an internal blog for comments and questions.

- Ask all participants within a training workshop to collaborate on best practices, using Google Docs.

- Use Twitter to create a backchannel for training questions and issues.

Finance and Administration

- Microblog your company's annual meeting.

- Add an investor-relations-oriented LinkedIn group that anyone can join.

- Consider which bloggers should be treated as financial analysts and media, and then treat them accordingly (e.g., add them to investor relations distribution lists, analyst briefings, etc.).

- Embed Social Media guidelines into all of the company's documentation (acceptable computer use policies, confidentiality policies, PR and media relations policies, etc.).

- If you are a public company, ask your attorneys for clarification regarding Social Media comments and participation prior to any financial announcement.

- Set a time and dollar budget for Social Media experimentation. And set a date when opportunistic experimentation ends and integrated planning begins.

- Ensure that any marketing- or advertising-based Social Media initiative is budgeted within that department.

- Ensure that any recruiting- or HR-based Social Media initiative is budgeted within that department.

- Decide on what baseline budget is required for ongoing compliance, technical support, and other shared costs.

- Ensure that a specific person and department are accountable for the budget planning.

- Read the fine print on each Social Media site to determine who owns the content and whether the Social Media site has the right to use the list of registrants for its own purposes.

- Assess the cost of moving the Social Media initiative from the proposed platform to a different one. (This might be done because of changed terms and conditions, risk of insolvency, purchase of the platform by a competitor, etc.)

- Assess the opportunity cost to the business in case the Social Media platform shuts down abruptly or in case the Social Media platform has a multi-hour (or multi-day) outage. Then plan for these contingencies, both operationally and financially.

Supply Chain and Production

- Set up a logistics on-time rating system for your industry.

- Set up a supplier quality-rating system for your industry.

- Connect consumer product ratings back to each supplier for quality assurance purposes.

- Solicit YouTube-type video proposals from suppliers; and set up an evaluation team to vote and comment on the proposals online.

- Use Twitter (or a private micro-blogging platform) to let distributors and wholesalers know about product issues and general delays.

- Solicit feedback directly from retailers about product issues, new product ideas, etc. (Normally the seller at the end of the supply chain is hidden from the manufacturer by distributors and other intermediaries.)

- Feed product quality information back into an online bidding system.

- Use Google Docs to collaborate with suppliers.

First Steps

1. Can you add to this list? Check out your competition, your customers, and your suppliers for ideas. Send us your ideas and we'll add to this list on the book's companion Web site.

2. It would never make sense to do everything on the list, but do some of the specific items make sense? Highlight these as possibilities for consideration in the next chapter.

16

Putting the Plan Together

There are four phases to any Social Media project: planning, implementation, monitoring, and evaluation. This chapter reviews planning and implementation; the next chapter reviews monitoring and evaluation.

Planning

The planning phase determines exactly what is being done, why, for whom, how it will be accomplished, and how it will be measured. The Social Media Priority Planner from Pinetree Advisors, shown a little later in this chapter, can be used as a guide.

Your company's Social Media strategy must always fit within the framework of your company's overall business strategy. While it is true that the unique nature of Social Media might mean that your company's overall business strategy should be *extended*, it shouldn't be *changed*. (If Social Media itself gets you rethinking about what your corporate strategy should be, then of course go back and revisit your strategy. Once it has been redefined, then come back to your Social Media strategy. Don't let the Social Media dog wag the corporate strategy tail!)

Define Social Media Audiences

Most companies interact with many different stakeholder groups: prospects, customers, employees, potential job candidates, shareholders, the media, and the general public. Even within each of these groups, there can be important subdivisions. Customers can be long-time customers or new ones. They can purchase one type of product or another. Their decision-makers can be younger or older. They can be major customers, or just occasional ones. They may be located in one region or national. And so on.

Whom do *you* wish to target with your Social Media initiative? While it's tempting to use a generic grouping, the tighter you can define your target, the clearer your message can be. As well, since different groups have different communication preferences, you need to build your initiative on the *right* Social Media platform, improving engagement even further.

On the other hand, if you are so narrow in your target definition, then you won't have enough critical mass. It's rarely worth it if you develop a Social Media initiative for just a handful of clients.

We recommend choosing two or three, or at most four, key target audiences.

Define Your Social Media Goals, by Audience

While some audiences may share the same goal, usually they are different—or at least nuanced. Some sample goals:

- To attract the best job candidates

- To build a customer-to-customer product support structure

- To generate buzz for new-product launches

- To reposition the brand for younger audiences

- To improve search engine ranking for specific keywords

- To collect implementation case studies from customers.

We've just recommended starting with audiences, then drilling down to goals. Sometimes companies find it easier to start with goals and then drill down to the audiences. In practice, it is an iterative process. Once the goals are set, you will need to review the audiences. (And if the goals are chosen first, then they may need to be revisited after the audiences are chosen.)

For each audience, there should be a detailed analysis:

- **Demographics:** Defining the demographics will later allow you to better match the Social Media platform to the group.

- **Behaviors:** Analyzing behaviors will help you identify where Social Media might fit into existing processes. For example, customers typically go through a purchase process that involves seeking recommendations from friends and colleagues. Since we know this, we might choose to build a recommendations system into our online store.

In addition, might there be a challenge that could prevent users from engaging in a Social Media initiative, or change the nature of their involvement? A simple example of this can be found by considering the teenager target group. They don't have laptops, but most carry a phone all day. For this group, a Web-based Social Media initiative will be far more effective if it had a strong mobile component.

> **Advanced Tip**
>
> *Whenever we've led focus groups, we've found that management's assumptions about their challenges are far different than the reality presented by the focus groups. Test your assumptions by convening a focus group; there's no downside, and it can significantly mitigate risks.*

- **Current challenges:** Try as it might, no company is absolutely perfect. Imagine that you had one of your target audience groups in a room and they were asked to identify your company's weaknesses. While not everything is fixable using Social Media, a few things would arise that could be addressed.

- **Personas:** This is one of the most powerful marketing techniques, and it applies perfectly in the Social Media world. A persona is a fictitious representative of a typical member of the group. Two examples—one for a person, one for a company:

  - **Jennifer:** In her early thirties, Jennifer divides her spare time between going to Starbucks, taking Yoga classes, and taking painting classes. She's an avid Facebook user, both keeping up with her family back home and connecting with her friends in the city. She works as a sales rep for Nike and is thrilled about her upcoming marriage.

  - **Northpark Fabrication:** Steady as she goes, Northpark has been a client for decades, maintaining a small but steady stream of sales. With 150 employees and centralized purchasing, the company has grown over 25 percent in the past two years. With new, younger management, they have begun buying from two out-of-state suppliers, and there is a risk that we might lose the account entirely.

By defining personas for each target group, marketing planners can ask how each persona would react to different marketing stimuli, and how each might

Advanced Tip

Personas are highly valuable beyond Social Media. The same personas can be used to evaluate your Web site and any other marketing or customer service initiative.

interact using a particular Social Media implementation. Think out loud: Would Jennifer be more likely to spend time on LinkedIn or Facebook?

If you're not sure where to start, then think of two typical customers in one of your target groups. Write down a description of the most salient points for each, then "average" them into a generic written description of the persona.

- **Target Social Media sites:** With a thorough understanding of each target group, the next question has to do with location. What Social Media sites would Jennifer (or Northpark) spend her time on? Sometimes this can be answered through market research or informal conversations; other times it can be answered by "lurking" on a particular site to assess the appropriateness yourself.

- **Messaging:** After the interaction on the site, what message would you want left with the participant? An interesting way to answer that question is to answer this one: If two people within your target group were talking about your company, what would you want them to be saying to each other? If you define it first, you can then consider the content that you would like to post and the type of interaction strategy. And if you wish, you can test for the message afterward in your market research.

- **Interaction strategy:** What precisely is the nature of the interaction that you are seeking to encourage? Typically, users follow a hierarchy of engagement. They're more likely to post a comment after they lurk for a while. They're more likely to tell their friends if they've first subscribed. And so on.

Figure 16.1 shows the seven levels of engagement, from low to high. Substitute the word trust for engagement, and this hierarchy illustrates something even more profound: the higher the trust, the more engagement—yet the more engagement, the higher the trust.

This is the point where you should identify specific ideas, campaigns, Web sites, etc. Chapter 15 provides many tactical examples that might be appropriate for you. Within the Social Media priority planner itself, we recommend putting a high-level description of what is proposed. Detailed specifications, project plans, and other material can be in a separate document.

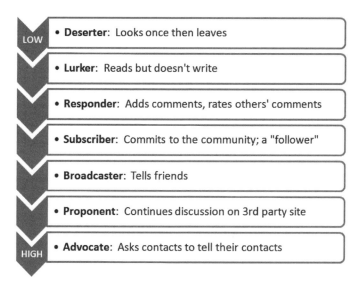

Figure 16.1. The seven levels of engagement in Social Media.

Benchmarks for Success

For each audience and goal, how will you know you are successful? In the early days of the Internet, success was measured foolishly with "eyeballs." Benchmarks need to be tied more deeply to your business goals and objectives. Several examples:

- Increase online sales by 10 percent.

- Reduce the number of unqualified candidates who are screened out by 20 percent over the previous year.

- Increase the unaided recall of our products' key benefits by 50 percent.

- Increase the number of registrants or followers by 20 percent.

- Reduce inbound telephone support calls by 30 percent.

In the next chapter, we explore ROI and measurement more fully.

Overall goal:

Audience:	Target Group 1	Target Group 2	Target Group 3	Target Group 4
Goals:				
Demographics:				
Behaviors:				
Current Challenges:				
Persona Description:				
Target Social Media Sites:				
Messaging:				
Interaction Strategy:				
Benchmark for Success:				
Risks/Mitigation Strategies				

Figure 16.2. Social media priority planner.

Risks

When something can go wrong, it will. The question is, will you be ready to handle it? Given the strategies that you've chosen, what are the likely areas of risk? If it is a contest, can people game the system somehow, to give them an unfair advantage? If it's a blog, can they write inflammatory comments? If it's a product-rating site, will you allow bad reviews and poor ratings? Planning how you will handle these (and other) risks—and how they can be mitigated in the first place—means that you will be better prepared to actually manage the initiative. And if you have chosen to outsource any part of it, your instructions will be that much clearer.

The goal of the Social Media priority planner (Figure 16.2), isn't to generate paperwork. The goal is to help you think through the plan strategically, and then get your entire team completely aligned. Most importantly, it is to make sure that your Social Media activities align with your overall corporate objectives.

Implementation

Choosing how to implement your strategy is a question that always comes up. Should it be added to a central group's responsibilities, such as marketing or IT? Does the company even have the expertise and the bandwidth for any development? Should a different group do the development than the ongoing management and monitoring? Should parts of it be outsourced, and if so, to whom: an ad agency, a contractor, or someone cheap overseas?

Every company is different. They have different industries, different in-house skills, different budgets, different priorities, and different goals. To suggest that there is one exclusive answer doesn't recognize the uniqueness of your company. Nevertheless, some of the factors to consider, and some general recommendations, are discussed next.

Do the Work Internally

Nobody knows your company the way you and your colleagues do. No matter how clever the consultant, agency, or contractor, he or she can't possibly brew all of your collective wisdom into the perfect implementation. And once the outsiders finish their work and leave, there is little or no knowledge transfer. Doing the work internally builds internal capability, and since there are no professional fees involved, this alternative is far less expensive.

Doing the work internally also brings some other benefits: There is more direct project control, and midcourse corrections are also easier. In addition, development can be extended from any experimental early-stage initiative projects that were already underway.

Outsource the Work

The best part about working with external people is that they "do" the job full-time, and they have developed an expertise and efficiency that can speed development—and reflect positively on your brand. Because they work for many different organizations, they bring their knowledge of best practices to the engagement, significantly improving the likelihood of success.

The reality of outsourcing in the Social Media world, however, is that the field is still relatively new, there are a significant number of platforms to learn, and there are very few real experts. You may find that your internal development team is as up-to-speed on the technology as anyone out there.

On the other hand, most organizations manage information technology (and marketing) budgets very tightly, and there aren't extra hours available for additional development projects; outsourcing is simply a pragmatic way to speed development. If you are hoping to do a very specialized development project, such as developing a Facebook or iPhone app, then your only real choice may be to outsource to a specialist in that technology.

One option that often is highly appealing is to outsource to developers in a cheaper country on the other side of the world. Indeed, entire Web sites are devoted to matching developers with clients—check out *www.elance.com, www.guru.com,* or *www.odesk.com.* The benefit of this type of outsourcing is the lower price tag. The challenge is that the contractor usually is not fluent in English and works in a time zone that is completely out of sync. What is gained in cost savings may be lost in the communication gap and the time zone. Be careful: If you are using an agency or consulting firm to manage the project, make sure you have a project manager that you trust, and that they are physically in your time zone—or close to it.

Launch Strategies

Once you've figured out the *what*, the next question is *how* the plan should be implemented. There are two different approaches to doing so: a gradual ramp-up and a big-bang launch.

Gradual Ramp-up

Trust is built one step at a time, over time. If part of your strategy is to develop trust for your senior executives or company spokespersons, then this can't be done in an instant. It is tempting to consider the authority of a title (CEO, president, VP, etc.) as conferring trust; it helps, but a title goes only part of the way. Having others comment on your credibility, vote on the usefulness of your comments, or come to your defense in a debate confers an entirely different level of trust. Having a large number of posts does so as well, as it confirms your longer-term interest and expertise in the subject under discussion, and a respect for the culture of the discussion group or blog.

The same can be said when your company plays host to an industry discussion group. The longer the group remains, the greater the forum's legitimacy—and yours. Again, time is a factor.

Gradual ramp-ups can also be used to stealthily begin a buzz about your company (or its products) on the ground.

Big-bang Launch:

Most marketing is campaign-driven: a new product launch, new corporate branding, and increased PR are typical campaign examples. When this is the case, Social Media can be used to amplify the campaign's message, extend the message over a greater time period, and attract third-party endorsement through user engagement.

Big-bang launches can also be used when traditional communications is used to drive traffic to a time-limited Social Media campaign. Typical examples of this are contests where the public is asked to create a video about your product, and others are asked to vote to choose a winner. In this case, both Social Media and traditional advertising would be used first to drive video creators, and then to drive the voters. (This type of campaign is also viral, as the video producers themselves have a strong incentive to drive their networks to vote.)

Other corporate activities that are big-bang candidates include recruiting and financial reporting—anything that works on a schedule.

Of course, the truth is that a comprehensive Social Media plan needs elements of both approaches. The low-level awareness and the gradual build-up is the fertile ground that helps leverage the "big-bang" launches.

Two activities that never work on a schedule are crisis management and crisis communications. Imagine that your product was implicated in a terrible accident: How could Social Media be used? On one hand, the immediacy of the response requires a big-bang approach. Yet, the credibility of your spokesperson, earned over a longer period of time, may just make the difference.

Choosing an Agency or Consultant

One of the great frustrations that many companies feel is when their agency or consultant doesn't deliver. There are a number of reasons this may happen, most of them preventable. Here are some:

- **The wrong consultants or agencies bid for the work**: Many organizations choose their vendors through a competitive bidding process. They put out a request for proposal, wait for the proposals to come in, choose a short list, listen to presentations, and finally select the lucky winner.

    The problem is that the most qualified vendors are often too busy to bother submitting a proposal. Even when they're not that busy, many will see the cost of participating in the process as too high, and the probability of winning too low, especially when there are a large number of bidders. For the most-qualified consultants and agencies, it's a sellers' market. For the least-qualified, it's a buyers' market.

    Solution: Until the market cools off, choose a trusted advisor who is an expert, and negotiate with him or her. If you don't have someone who fits the role, look for organizations that have a track record, and invite a very small number of them in to talk about your project. An unscripted conversation is a small investment that most vendors should be willing to make, and it allows you to test-drive the relationship before asking them to put together a proposal.

- **The consultant or agency is learning on the job:** There is no shortage of "false prophets" who do not have the depth of experience to do the work, but who are smart enough to stay one step ahead of their prospective clients. As a result, your project may experience delays and cost overruns.

  Solution: To protect yourself, make sure that the terms of your engagement letter reflect the value of the learning that the consultant is gaining by working on your project. If this isn't the case, avoid the problem by asking detailed questions about their Social Media history over the past five to ten years, and verify it through reference checks. If the vendor has a long-time relationship with you, is honest about a lack of knowledge, and you still want them to do the job, then it shouldn't be unexpected when you encounter surprises.

- **Costs are spiraling; project is delayed:** Often this is caused by poorly specified projects or midcourse changes by the client.

  Solution: Agree to the scope at the beginning of the project, and ask the vendor if the scope is detailed enough for them to provide a cost estimate with a high degree of certainty. Ensure that any changes to the budget and schedule are signed off by both parties along the way. If budget is a critical factor, engage the vendor on a fixed-price basis.

- **Bait and switch:** Often, the senior person (who is the Social Media expert) is involved in the marketing and sales process, but once the contract is signed, the work delivery is delegated to a fairly junior team member. This means that you need to spend time bringing this person up to speed. And when they do begin the engagement, you really have the benefit of only their limited experience, not the senior person's.

  Solution: Ensure that anyone involved in the business-development process will also be involved day-to-day in the project execution. Insist that the project manager be involved from day one.

General Recommendations

During the planning process, include external resources, such as your agency or consultant, as you are looking to get as much best-practices and "outside of the box" thinking as possible. Depending on the strength of the relationship, and their company knowledge, you may wish to grant them more or less responsibility for the planning process itself.

If you do not have enough internal bandwidth for development, we recommend that it also be outsourced, but with the proviso that knowledge transfer, in one form or another, be part of the contracted engagement. Implementation should be handled internally as much as possible. Unlike other marketing projects that are more broadcast in nature, the conversational nature of Social Media means that only internal people can really speak for the organization. The only exception to this might be the clerical posting of certain items throughout different Social Media networks, which often can be cheaply outsourced abroad. (An example of this might be the cross-posting of press release headlines on Twitter, which sometimes can't be automated.)

Social Media monitoring (discussed in the next chapter) should be part of the standard monitoring that is done across any marketing initiative, and it should be done no differently. The only caveat is that some of the monitoring isn't just statistical analytics, but actually reviewing conversations in real time—a qualitative exercise that can't always be outsourced.

First Steps

1. This is the chapter where your plan is formulated. Sometimes it is tough to figure it out; if this is the case for you, consider re-reading the book to consolidate your knowledge, or ask a trusted advisor to give you his or her perspective.

2. The most important chart in the entire book is the Social Media Priority Planner. Even if you already "know" what you're going to do, spend some time documenting it in the chart. If you can't fill in the blanks, then you are proving that the effort is tough to justify—and may be unfocused as well.

17

ROI and Measurement

Are you listening? With Social Media, people are talking about you; they are spreading the word on you, your products, your brand, your business (good and bad). They are posting videos and comments, rating you, reviewing you, including you in blog posts, tweeting about you, and recommending you (or not). Some of the Social Media conversation you instigated on purpose, while some you had nothing to do with starting.

Social Media measurement and analysis is in a very confusing place right now, but it is important to get a handle on knowing what's being said, where it's being said, by whom it is being said, and what impact this is having on your business. For the activities you instigated, you need to measure the impact and determine if you could improve this or, if you're not getting the results you had anticipated, decide where you could better spend your time and money to improve your results.

Some of our Social Media measurements will be fairly easy and some very difficult.

Return on Investment

Return on investment (ROI) is a relatively simple concept. You make an investment (of time or money or both) and you hope to get something valuable in return: sales, visitors, friends (on Facebook, not the real kind ☺), fans, followers. . . .

Sometimes this calculation is easy and straightforward. You run a sponsored listing campaign in Google to sell seats at an event and develop a unique **landing page**. The cost to run this ad is $100. The sales from this landing page are 10 sales at $1,000 each. Your cost per person for the event is $150. The ROI is calculated as:

Landing page

A page, usually with special messaging, that is arrived at through a link in an advertisement.

$$ROI = \frac{(\text{Gain from Investment} - \text{Cost of Investment})}{\text{Cost of Investment}}$$

In this case the gain is ($1,000 – $150) x 10 people, or $8,500. The cost of the investment (the Google ads) is $100. The ROI is (8,500 – 100)/100, or 8,400 percent.

The return on advertising dollars spent (or ROAS) is $84. This means that for every dollar of advertising, you are given back $84 in profit—not bad at all!

Sometimes the calculation is not so simple—you invested time in Facebook groups looking for and answering questions to create a presence and build your reputation as an expert in your field. You hoped that people who viewed the answer would click through to your page and ask to be a fan; then after they became fans they would be so wowed by your content that they would click through to your Web site and order your product. Hmmm, not so easy.

Social Media participation is not so difficult to measure. You can determine the number of visitors to your site from your YouTube videos, and from there you can determine their specific actions if you are using the right traffic-analysis programs.

With Social Media ROI, most people don't know where to start. We recommend that you start with the end in mind. What is it you want to accomplish? Quantify it. Where are you now? Know your baseline before you start.

With Social Media we definitely need to consider the return on effort (ROE) as well. The amount of time we spend on Social Media is time that we could be spending in other ways and through other venues to achieve our objectives. Today it is critically important to keep track of the amount of time you spend in each of the Social Media venues you participate in on a regular basis. There are tools to help you with this: Rescue Time (*http://www.rescuetime.com*) is a good example.

Sometimes when we look at the results of our Social Media efforts we are not as interested in the numbers themselves as we are in what those numbers lead to—are we more interested in the number of Twitter followers we have or the number of purchases made by our Twitter followers?

In Social Media marketing, sometimes we need to stop looking at things on a granular level and take a broader approach.

Several Approaches

Right now businesses are taking several approaches to Social Media marketing.

- Larger companies with a significant Social Media investment and a budget for Social Media measurement are trying to get a handle on the return they are getting on their Social Media investment. Some of these are using services like Nielsen BuzzMetrics, Cymphony Verismo, and Techrigy SM2 and are supplementing this with internal analysis.

- Some companies are trying to do their analysis internally through a combination of traditional Web traffic analysis and Web metrics tools, as well as some of the recently developed tools that focus on engagement, sentiment, and other important factors related specifically to Social Media.

- Some companies are taking a broader, very simplistic view and looking at things on a macro level. They know what their traditional marketing has brought them in the past. The new things they are doing are all related to Social Media. So they look at the difference between the latest stats and their (prior-year's) benchmark stats to see the impact of their Social Media efforts.

Before You Start

To have any meaningful measurement and analysis, you need to know your starting point so you can measure the results of your Social Media marketing. You will want basic statistics like:

- Number of Facebook friends and fans

- Number of LinkedIn connections

- Number of Twitter followers

- Number of YouTube subscribers

- Traffic stats

- Digg links

- Stats from any other Social Media sites you currently use.

You will also want stats on the things that will be impacted by your Social Media objectives, resulting in different Social Media strategies and Social Media marketing campaigns. Things like:

- Search engine ranking

- Dollars spent on customer service if one of your objectives is to reduce cost of delivery of customer service through Social Media

- Dollars (and time) spent on recruiters, if one of your objectives is to reduce the cost of candidate sourcing and recruiting

- Dollars spent on market research, if one of your objectives is to do market research through Social Media.

What Is Being Measured?

The performance of Social Media campaigns is sometimes analyzed using metrics like traffic, links, and comments. Sometimes more abstract measurements are analyzed—things like reviews, sentiment, rating, opinions, and buzz. What you choose to measure goes back to your goals and objectives, and what you wanted to receive in return for your investment of time or money.

Most objectives can be categorized into *exposure, engagement, influence,* and *action/results.* Some of the measurement tactics for each category include the following.

Exposure

- Search engine rank

- Unique visitors

- Increase in traffic

- Pay-per-click ad impressions.

Engagement

- Page views per visitor

- Time spent on site/blog/Social Media

- Click-throughs

- Repeat visitors

- Comments

- Messages

- Reviews

- Ranks

- Posts

- Social bookmarking

- Fans

- Followers

- Friends.

Influence

- Retweets

- Recommendations

- Bookmarks

- Sent to a friend

- Links to your site/blog/page.

Action/Results

- Purchases

- Leads

- Contacts

- Increase in sales

- Calls

- E-club sign-ups

- Conversions

- RSS subscriptions and track-backs

- Requests to be a fan/follower/friend

- Savings in customer service or market research

- Number of resumes submitted or number of candidates interviewed.

It is always important to remember that quality trumps quantity every time, so you want to take the quality of the results into consideration when looking at your results. It might be very easy to get 5,000 Twitter followers by using some of the automated tools, but they are of no value if they are not interested in your products and services and are just following you because you followed them.

We also have to realize that things like mentions are not a deep enough statistic for most of our purposes. We need to know the sentiment—how many mentions were positive, and how many mentions were negative? The same is true of followers and fans, where the number alone doesn't necessarily give us valuable information relative to our Social Media strategy. The number of followers, friends, or fans is not as important as the quality, engagement, and actions of these followers, friends, and fans.

You also must take into consideration that the results from Social Media participation and the ability to measure them are not as immediate as most traditional Web traffic analysis and metrics. We have to give it time and take that into consideration. It takes time to build a relationship, and it is difficult to measure the value of that relationship.

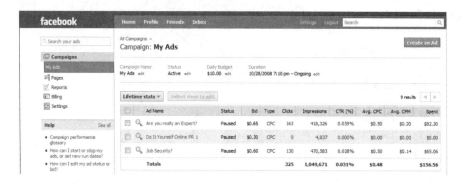

Figure 17.1. Facebook Insights provides analytics relating to your social ads and Facebook page.

Stats from Social Media Platforms

Many of the Social Media venues provide you with stats. Facebook Insights (Figure 17.1) provides details on user exposure, actions, and behavior relating to your social ads and Facebook page. The figure gives some visibility to three ads in a campaign. Clearly, one was far less successful than the others in generating impressions and clicks.

Page admins also have the ability to see information about their fan base and the fans who interact with their content. Facebook provides access to demographic data (such as age and gender) and geographic data (such as country, city, and spoken language) when there are a significant number of fans in each statistical category.

Flickr provides stats to its Pro members.

YouTube also has fairly robust statistics (Figure 17.2). The figure shows one of Randall Craig's channels.

We have provided information on stats in each of the Social Media venue sections of this book.

Additional Resources

Here are some additional resources that you may find useful.

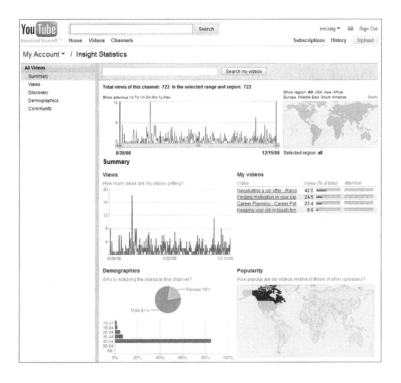

Figure 17.2. YouTube provides valuable stats on views, demographics, popularity, and other useful criteria.

Software/Tools

There are many tools available to help us with various aspects of Social Media measurement.

- Google Alerts (*http://www.google.com/alerts*) will send you an email alert every time your business or your products are mentioned on the Web, in the news, in a blog, or in a video description.

- Google Analytics (*http:www.google.com/analytics*) is designed to provide visibility for Web site traffic. It should be used both within your blog and within your Web site. The stats will show you the source of each user and will help you understand the traffic (and efficiency) from each Social Media site source.

- HootSuite (*http://www.hootsuite.com*) provides tracking and measurement stats related to your Twitter activity.

- Viralheat (*http://www.viralheat.com*) provides Social Media monitoring, analytics, and insights with location filtering.

- Crimson Hexagon (*http://www.crimsonhexagon.com*) has two products—VoxTrot Buzz which shows the volume of mentions and sentiment, and VoxTrot Opinion which goes deeper into online sentiment.

- Radian6 (*http://www.radian6.com*) (see Figure 17.3) enables you to slice, segment, filter, and parse your Social Media data to view and measure through dozens of lenses.

- Sentiment Metrics (*http://www.sentimentmetrics.com*) gathers mentions of your brand, analyzes the data, and presents it in a meaningful format.

Figure 17.3. Radian6 enables you to slice and dice your Social Media data for relevant and detailed analysis.

- Tweet Feel (*http://www.tweetfeel.com*) provides a free tool where you input your brand and it provides the tweets that mention the term, as well as the percentage positive and the percentage negative. They also have a Tweet Feel Biz that takes the monitoring and feedback to a much higher level.

- Bit.ly (*http://www.bit.ly*) and several other URL shorteners also have stats that show you how much (and from where) traffic comes to your blog or Web site.

- TweetReach (*http://www.tweetreach.com*) (see Figure 17.4) shows you how far your Tweet has traveled.

- Susan and Randall are always updating their social bookmarks with great tools and resources. Check them out at Diigo:

  - Susan's are available at *www.diigo.com/user/susansweeney*.

  - Randall's are available at *www.diigo.com/user/RandallCraig*.

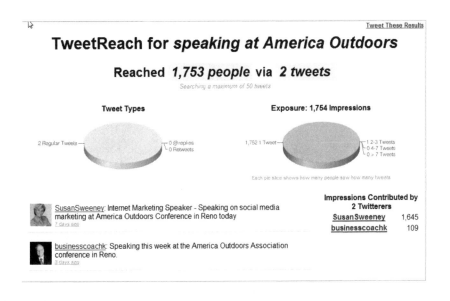

Figure 17.4. TweetReach is an online tool that shows your Tweet's exposure.

Articles

- An excellent article from Mashable on measuring Social Media ROI can be found at *http://budurl.com/chapter17roi.*

- A list (a Wiki, actually) from Ken Burbary, with over 100 Social Media monitoring solutions, can be found at *http://budurl.com/chapter17wiki.*

Education

- Susan has ongoing live webinars and recorded online courses on this topic available through the webinars and online store at her site, *http://www.susansweeney.com*, and provides access to others' courses on the subject through her online learning portal, eLearningU, at http://www.elearningu.com.

- Randall delivers workshops and webinars on this and related Social Media topics, all available at *www.RandallCraig.com.*

18

Keeping Up-to-Date

The pace of change and the degree of innovation in Social Media are alarmingly fast. Not a day goes by without another new service, Web site, or mobile innovation being announced. At the same time, many sites are forging partnerships, connections, and data-sharing deals with what used to be their competition. And data (including comments and ratings) are being syndicated and used in ways that were never expected initially.

To try to keep up-to-date on everything in the Social Media world is more than a full-time job, so it is tempting either to dive in completely (and begin ignoring your "real" business) or to pretend that change never happens (and therefore miss key opportunities to connect with your stakeholders). Thankfully, there is a middle ground, once your initial strategy is in place:

Learn from Your Network

The underlying purpose of Social Media is to connect outward to prospects, clients, suppliers, job candidates, former employees, the media, and sometimes the general public, among others. All of these groups are using Social Media already, and all of them are being told by their networks about new Social Media sites and applications. Why not tap into this rich vein of knowledge, and ask them what they know and what they are learning? Here are some ideas:

- Using the formal market research that you already do (e.g., focus groups, interviews, surveys), add several questions about Social Media usage patterns and interesting new Social Media sites.

- Ask your sales team to informally ask their prospects and clients about Social Media usage during their sales calls. Ask them to find out what would be helpful to this group.

- Ask your supply chain team (e.g., purchasers, logistics managers, etc.) to informally ask their outside contacts as well.

- Create an optional survey on your Web site.

- Ask the question in your company blog.

- Ask the question within a Tweet.

- Review comments posted within your Social Media initiatives.

There is almost a beauty to finding out about Social Media using Social Media; you are using the tool precisely for what it is supposed to be used for. Once the data is in, you will then have a universe of information that can be organized, culled, and investigated.

Learn from Your (Younger) Staff

If you've ever spent time with teenagers and "kids" in their twenties, you'll notice that they spend a huge amount of time living in the Social Media world. Their Facebook updates automatically appear on their cell phones. Computer games aren't fun unless they are doing them with other people—even people they don't know from the other side of the world. Pictures they take with their phones are automatically uploaded to Flickr. And so on.

While you may be very comfortable with spreadsheets, word processing, and email, have you ever tried to explain the underlying concepts to a person who wasn't computer savvy? (Or, worse, tried to explain an operating system, applications, and files?)

In the same way that these people don't have any idea of what might be possible using these tools, so too might the same be said today about Social Media. Even though YouTube, Facebook, and LinkedIn have made it easy, the technical possibilities are often beyond the ken of the typical 40-year-old decision maker.

At the same time, the commercial possibilities are often beyond the ken of the typical 25-year-old. For this reason, we strongly recommend that you canvass your younger staff for their experience. What sites and services are they using? What are their friends from other companies using? What is trending up (and down)? If you don't have younger employees, then canvass this age group outside of your organization. It is the synthesis of their Social Media savvy with your business acumen that can identify relevant and investment-worthy Social Media possibilities.

Learn from Your Investments

If you support an initiative on any of the major Social Media sites, subscribe to (and read!) these sites' own blogs. This is the best place to keep up-to-date with new features, integration with other platforms, and general best practices. Since you've already made an investment, it makes sense to leverage it as much as possible.

At the same time, look again at the general level of engagement among your target users: One of the best things you can do is to stop Social Media initiatives that are not working as well as expected, and redeploy your resources elsewhere.

Learn from the Internet

There is no shortage of Web sites, blogs, and discussion groups that can provide detailed Social Media minutiae, so-called best practices, Social Media news, and everything in between. Unfortunately, it is very difficult—and time consuming—to separate out the "trusted gurus" from the "false prophets." We recommend a two-pronged approach to Internet-based Social Media learning:

- Tactical problem solving: If you have a specific problem, or are investigating a potential opportunity, searching for it on Google often will yield the relevant answer. Most problems already have been solved somewhere, so often this is enough. If you have something specific that hasn't been answered, you need to balance the time required to ask your question/wait for the answer with calling your real-world Social Media consultant and getting the answer directly in your context.

- "What's new" information surfing: There are a number of news and comment-oriented Web sites and blogs that provide Social Media updates.

Some merely repurpose press releases, others provide detailed reviews, and still others provide an interesting running commentary. At the same time, some are aimed at the general public, others at a technical audience, and others at a marketing audience. An updated list of some of these is available on this book's companion Web site, as well as on the authors' resource sites. If you are interested in a well-rounded Social Media news summary, look at *www.mashable.com*; we've provided direct links to a number of their specialized pages within the Resources section of relevant chapters. Of course, following @randallcraig and @susansweeney on Twitter will also give you some insights. Our blogs also discuss Social Media.

- There is a third approach, characterized as a "deep dive." Like all industries and functional areas, the Social Media community itself has endless discussions on the relative merits of different approaches, technical how-to's and work-arounds, as well as interesting examples of leading-edge marketing successes (and failures). Those in the industry as consultants (such as us) devote many, many hours participating in these conversations. Unless your company's business is Internet-driven, you probably won't have the time for this approach.

First Steps

Set aside time on your calendar each month or quarter to make sure that you're up-to-date on the latest innovations and best practices. If you don't want to do the research yourself, then find a trusted advisor who can give you a briefing on it.

About the Authors

Susan Sweeney, CA, CSP, HoF

Renowned Internet marketing expert, consultant, best-selling author, and speaker Susan Sweeney, CA, CSP, HoF, tailors lively keynote speeches and full- and half-day seminars and workshops for companies, industries, and associations interested in improving their Internet presence and increasing their Internet traffic and sales.

Susan has developed many Internet projects over the years—her latest is eLearningU (*www. eLearningU.com*), a comprehensive online learning site. Susan is a partner of Verb Interactive, an international Web development, Internet marketing and consulting firm. She holds both the Chartered Accountant and Certified Speaking Professional designations. Susan has been inducted into the Canadian Speakers Hall of Fame.

Susan is the author of many books on Internet marketing and e-business: *101 Ways to Promote Your Web Site* (a best seller with over 77,000 copies sold, now in its eighth edition; it has been translated into German and Spanish), *101 Internet Businesses You Can Start from Home, Internet Marketing for Your Tourism Business, 3G Marketing on the Internet, The e-Business Formula for Success,* and *Going for Gold.* She is also the developer of a two-day intensive Internet Marketing Boot Camp. Susan offers many Web-based teleseminars, seminars on CD, and e-books related to Internet marketing.

Susan is a member of the Canadian Association of Professional Speakers, the National Speakers Association, and the Global Speakers Federation.

Verb Interactive is a marketing firm that provides Web development and Internet marketing, consulting, and training services to industry and government. Their primary services include Web site design and development, Internet marketing strategies and campaigns, SEO, Web site report cards, Internet marketing consulting, and competitive analysis.

Susan has been sharing her vast Internet marketing expertise with corporate and conference audiences around the globe for over 10 years. Susan's passion for the subject, her depth of knowledge, and her enthusiasm fuel her dynamic presentations. To discuss hiring Susan to speak for your next event or having her do a private Internet Marketing Bootcamp for your organization, contact her speaking office at 1-888-274-0537, or to find out about Susan's upcoming webinars, her Internet Marketing Bootcamps, her latest e-books and podcasts, or to sign up for her newsletter, visit her Web site at *http://www.susansweeney.com.*

Contact information
    Susan Sweeney, CA, CSP, HoF
    www.susansweeney.com
    www.verbinteractive.com
    susan@susansweeney.com
    Phone: 888-274-0537
    www.LinkedIn.com/in/SusanSweeneycsp
    twitter.com/susansweeney
    www.diigo.com/user/susansweeney
    www.facebook.com/susan.sweeney01
    www.youtube.com/SusanSweeneyInternet

Randall Craig, CFA, MBA, CMC

Randall Craig is an Internet pioneer who has led the Web strategies for several major market newspapers, international financial institutions, and consulting firms since 1994. He speaks and consults on Social Media strategy and policy with clients and uses it extensively himself.

Over his career, Randall has founded several successful start-ups, held a long-time position at a "big-four" consulting firm, and was a senior executive at an American public company. He is currently the president of the consulting firm Pinetree Advisors (*www.ptadvisors.com*), leading a team that specializes in Web and Social Media strategy. His focus, both as a speaker and as a consultant, is on professional service firms, media/publishing, associations, education, and financial services.

Over the past 24 years, he has served over 100 major clients on substantive projects, and as a professional speaker has given hundreds of presentations on this topic. Over the past five years, he has been profiled or quoted in over 400 newspaper, radio, and TV interviews.

Randall is the author of numerous books including *Leaving the Mother Ship* and the best-seller and award-winning *Personal Balance Sheet.* He is also the author of both *Online PR and Social Media for Experts* and *Online PR and Social Media for Associations and Not-for-Profits.* Randall writes a weekly column on the Monster career site, hosts the weekly WebTV show *Professionally Speaking TV* (*www.ProfessionallySpeakingTV.com*), and lectures at the Schulich School of Business.

Randall is the 2010 Toronto chapter president of the Canadian Association of Professional Speakers and is a member of the Global Speakers Federation. He has a CFA, MBA, CMC, and a black belt in karate.

Randall's high-energy presentations on Social Media are highly customized and up-to-date: Depending on your needs, they can demystify, brainstorm, strategize, identify risks, entertain, or talk tech. No matter the goal, Randall's presentations are real and practical—not theoretical. To discuss hiring Randall to speak at your next event, consult on Social Media strategy, or perform a Social Media effectiveness audit, contact him at 416-256-7773 or *www.RandallCraig.com*.

Contact information
Randall Craig, CFA, MBA, CMC
www.randallcraig.com
www.ptadvisors.com
request@RandallCraig.com
Phone: 416-256-7773
www.LinkedIn.com/in/RandallCraig
Twitter.com/randallcraig
www.diigo.com/user/RandallCraig
www.facebook.com/Randall.Craig

Index

Reader Feedback Sheet

Your comments and suggestions are very important in shaping future publications. Please e-mail us at *info@maxpress.com* or photocopy this page, jot down your thoughts and mail it to:

Maximum Press

Attn: Jim Hoskins

605 Silverthorn Road

Gulf Breeze, FL 32561

_____

_____

_____

_____

_____

_____

_____

_____

_____

_____

_____

_____

_____

_____

_____

_____

_____

_____

_____

_____

_____

***101 Ways to Promote
Your Web Site,
Seventh Edition***
by Susan Sweeney, C.A.
392 pages
$29.95
ISBN: 978-1-931644-65-5

***101 Internet Businesses
You Can Start From Home
Second Edition***
by Susan Sweeney, C.A.
336 pages
$29.95
ISBN: 978-1-931644-48-8

***3G Marketing on the
Internet,
Seventh Edition***
by Susan Sweeney, C.A.,
Andy MacLellen & Ed
Dorey
216 pages
$34.95
ISBN: 978-1-931644-37-2

Podcasting for Profit
by Leesa Barnes
376 pages
$34.95
ISBN: 978-1-931644-57-0

To purchase a Maximum Press book, visit your local bookstore,
call (850) 934-4583 or visit *maxpress.com* for online ordering.